AF379968

My
Selfie
with
Integrity

Arun Kumar Jagatramka is a chartered accountant with an All India First Rank and Gold Medal. He is the chairman of Gujarat NRE Group, one of the largest independent producers of metallurgical coke, and a wealth creator of India.

He has been a member of the India–Australia CEO Forum and the India–Japan Business Leaders Forum nominated by the prime minister of India. He has also served as the honorary NSW Sydney ambassador to India, appointed by the government of New South Wales, Australia.

He is an active and a prominent member of the Confederation of Indian Industry (CII), the Associated Chambers of Commerce and Industry of India (ASSOCHAM), etc. and a coveted speaker at national and international platforms like Horasis, Coaltrans, Carbon Forum, Met Coke World on a wide range of subjects like economy, industry, steel, coking coal, met coke, ethics, integrity and corruption in India.

He is the founder of Gujarat NRE–AMA Centre for National Integrity at the Ahmedabad Management Association. He is also the former chairman of the ASSOCHAM National Council on Ease of Doing Business.

My *Selfie* with Integrity

and the Gujarat NRE story

Arun Kumar Jagatramka

Picture Abhi Baaki Hai Mere Dost!

RUPA

Published by
Rupa Publications India Pvt. Ltd 2020
7/16, Ansari Road, Daryaganj
New Delhi 110002

Sales Centres:
Allahabad Bengaluru Chennai
Hyderabad Jaipur Kathmandu
Kolkata Mumbai

Copyright © Arun Kumar Jagatramka, 2020

The views and opinions expressed in this book are the author's own and the
facts are as reported by him which have been verified to the extent possible,
and the publishers are not in any way liable for the same.

All rights reserved.
No part of this publication may be reproduced, transmitted,
or stored in a retrieval system, in any form or by any means,
electronic, mechanical, photocopying, recording or otherwise,
without the prior permission of the publisher.

Revised Edition 2020
This edition is the revised version in compliance of the order dated 21.10.2020 passed by
Hon'ble Delhi High Court which vacated the injunction granted on the release of 1st edition of
this book in the Appeal preferred by the author.

ISBN: 978-93-89967-32-6

First impression 2020

10 9 8 7 6 5 4 2 3 1

The moral right of the author has been asserted.

Disclaimer: This book is the next step in the author's quest for an India free from
corruption. No malice or accusation is intended.

Printed at Nutech Print Services India

This book is sold subject to the condition that it shall not, by way
of trade or otherwise, be lent, resold, hired out, or otherwise circulated,
without the publisher's prior consent, in any form of binding or
cover other than that in which it is published.

যদি তোর ডাক শুনে কেউ না আসে
তবে একলা চলো রে!
—রবীন্দ্রনাথ ঠাকুর (গুরুদেব)

'If your call is unheeded,
walk alone!'

—Rabindranath Tagore (Gurudev)

CONTENTS

ACKNOWLEDGEMENTS

While I have been battling corruption in India for over a decade, there are a few intelligent and knowledgeable people without whom none of it would have been possible.

The first person that I would like to thank, is my father the late Girdharilal Jagatramka, who set an example for me with his actions of never bending down to the evils of corruption, and gave me the weapons of education and justice, so that I could fight my way out of the corrupt quagmire.

My wife Mona for her strength, wisdom, and empathy shall always have my love and respect.

My children for understanding, supporting, and furthering my quest for integrity shall always have my love and pride. I would like to especially thank my eldest Tanvee for helping me write this book.

I would like to express my gratitude to the venerable D. R. Kaarthikeyan, without whom it would have been very difficult to further my dream of demolishing corruption in India, and meet the stalwarts of our country who have been working against corruption.

I would like to thank Bipin Newar for helping me find the most supportive and understanding publishing house Rupa.

Finally, I would like to thank everyone at Rupa, in particular Raju Barman, and my editor Dibakar Ghosh for their patient introduction and guidance to the world of publishing.

PROLOGUE

A popular Hindi song proclaims:

'मुर्गी क्या जाने अंडे का क्या होगा?'

'Does the Chicken know the Egg's destiny?'

Life is unpredictable. Like the pages of an exciting mystery novel, with each turn of a page it reveals something new and unexpected. For me, this uncertainty is what makes 'living' a beautiful adventure.

As I sit at my desk, penning my random thoughts on paper, or rather typing on my laptop … a motion picture with a running time of 50+ years envelops my mind; the highs and the lows, the friends and the foes, the victories and the failures—each frame of the storyboard passes before my eyes like film on an old-fashioned projector, and makes me more excited for the rest. Because rest assured पिक्चर अभी बाकी है मेरे दोस्त!

This is not an autobiography. I still have a lot of plans and projects to get through before I even think about retirement. This is a pen portrait of my memoirs. My exploration of life as I have lived it. The events that have shaped me and my present, the mistakes and failures that taught me valuable lessons, the demons and mountains that challenged me and how I overcame them, the love and respect that I earned through sheer hard work and honesty.

It is the story of a common man who challenged the corrupt system and refused to bend down to its mores. It is a recollection of memories and events that made Integrity a part of my daily life and corruption my arch-nemesis. If the story of a simple middle-class boy who grew up to become a simple billionaire—his integrity still intact—interests you, dear reader, then come along.

1

MIDDLE CLASS BEGINNINGS

I wonder where should I begin my tale. From the cold December night when I bawled and kicked my way into the world, or should I jump into the mini-series of disconnected anecdotes and experiences through which corruption trickled into my conscious teenage brain, trying to pulverise its innocence. The former would be rather boring and cumbersome, I imagine because I had the typical middle-class childhood and upbringing as almost everyone around me. My regular childhood did not really lend itself to my quest for a corruption-free India. The latter I think would be too random with kangaroo-like leaps into the timeline of my life to make any sense, leading to confusion and innumerable head-scratches. Let me try and show you the highlights—the specific events; the choices that I, and those around me made; and the experiences that moved and moulded me—that instigated within me the drive to find solutions for an India full of integrity.

The person who demands precedence in my story above all others—the one who taught me the value of honesty and integrity, who guided me to become a successful person, and who stood by me, when the world seemed to have forsaken me—is my father, Girdharilal Jagatramka. The quintessential middle-class Indian, my father had made the vast city of Calcutta his home. He was born in British-colonised India, witnessed India's Tryst with Destiny, and suffered through the cleave that was the Partition of India. Perhaps, having lived through such momentous events of history, he was a man much ahead of his time.

More than anybody else, he understood the power and importance of a strong education—irrespective of gender. He enrolled us, first in a Hindi-medium school, as was the norm of the day, but then showing incredible foresight and confidence in my abilities he had me transferred to an English-medium school towards the end of my primary level education. Suddenly

I found myself sitting in my first History lecture delivered completely in the then foreign and bewildering to me, English. That first lecture, I sat, surrounded by new and more confident faces, wondering what was a cricket umpire doing in the middle of Rome in AD 50. You see at that time I did not know the difference between an umpire and an empire!

I was never a fan of homework or revisions; what kid is? I gathered information and knowledge from unconventional sources—from conversations around me, from newspapers, from my family's discussions of current affairs and their opinions, from thriller and mystery novels, and the biggest source of learning, if you will believe it, was cinema. I grew up on a daily diet of blockbuster 70s Hindi cinema—learning the complexities of the human condition through the emotions and drama splattered across the huge 70 mm canvas—watched with sneaky relish. But more than anything I earned knowledge through unabashedly asking questions. Much, much before I had turned even eighteen, I was enrolled into my father's office. Now along with my academic pursuits, I was responsible for the accounts-book of my father's company. This I did with pleasure, as I enjoyed playing with numbers and I was getting firsthand knowledge of the day-to-day activities and mode of working in a business environment.

My probably prescient, I suspect, and cautionary father wanted me to be an independent professional, and not join the family business. Not because my family business was some Godfather-like mafia, but perhaps he could gauge the ups and downs and the difficulties that a young India's industry would suffer from, due to changing government regulations—namely the different 'rajs' (licence, raid, etc.) that the Indian government had split in lieu of the British Raj. Like every parent, he wanted to cushion me from uncertainties and frustrations. But, *murgi kya jaane ande ka kya hoga?* But I am getting ahead of myself.

So I chose to work towards a Chartered Accountant's Certificate. Now with my studies added to my responsibilities as the accountant of my father's company, my plate was full. Thus, along with theory I was also getting first-hand knowledge of the practice that I needed. Perhaps this is the reason that in the examination where failures are more the norm than success, I, on my very first attempt secured the 'All India First Rank', Gold Medal. Because truth be told the day before the exam, you would have found me in the legendary Jyoti cinema watching the immensely gripping *Sholay*.

I have just realized that I have not presented a very good example for you. But perhaps my life is proof that rote learning and homework is not the way to success, but inquisitiveness, hard work, integrity and confidence in one's own ability and of course a strong and trusting parent is.

2

STEPPING OUT

My father's business was not as big as to warrant any raids or unscrupulous demands. Still the everyday corruption that we encountered made him the proud owner of several 3-inch thick files full of copies of letters that he had written to authorities complaining about the bribes being demanded for basic necessities like phones, gas, and banking—facilities. The ₹100 in exchange for the life-line of the very first clunky, shiny-black telephone that my father refused to produce; my harassed father, firmly standing his ground that it was his right to have access to his bank locker during regular business hours without coughing up a bribe, and if the officer in question did not relent, he would be forced to put a dead fish inside his locker (The threat did not help. Perhaps the fish-loving officer was confident that a pure-vegetarian man would rather jump into the Hooghly than touch the dead body of an animal); the endless letters that my father wrote to the then Minister of Petroleum because despite following the government-defined rules, the LPG dealer refused to deliver the LPG cylinder to our house without a bribe, the sum of which was larger than the gas connection itself—were commonplace and irked me, but I did not realize that corruption was such a malady that was disintegrating the very fabric of our society. Only after qualifying, when I stepped out of my father's cozy home, did the impact of corruption really start to jar me.

My first job outside my father's office was with a jolly man called Bhagirathji. My father's business was finance in various forms, and Bhagirathji was an old acquaintance and very knowledgeable in the same field. I started to spend my lunch hours in his office. And so every afternoon I learnt the basics of business and finance, and how work can be made more enjoyable when thongas of jhal muri is added to the mix. It was in his office that I first encountered 'raids'. At random, without any prior notice or indication, a team of men would descend—overflowing with demands. The real seemingly only motive for the uninvited and undesired imposition—cash.

But Bhagirathji was always a step ahead of them. He did not keep a single banknote in the office.

Demonetization is a very recent event that has stamped itself into our history. But early in the 1980s, Bhagirathji illustrated the beauty of not carrying or hoarding large amounts of cash in our corruption-oriented economy. The 'government officers'—disgruntled, would disrupt the entire working day, but in the end leave, empty-handed.

And so, I learnt to always conduct business through cheques and bank transfers. Even when, inevitably cash had to be involved, I always acquired legal paperwork for it. I was determined to not give in to the pain and shame that the innumerable Rajs had been designed for.

Bhagirathji used to get outsourced work from Birla House—the head office of the Birlas'. Thus, he personally knew Mr K. K. Birla. Perhaps on his recommendation, I was handpicked by the eminent businessman to handle his personal finances. It was a great opportunity for a fresher like me with no mentors in sight. The very first day that I took up my role in my new office, dressed carefully in my brand new safari suit—they were the clothes de rigueur at the time—and my hair strictly combed back, I was trying to look like a veteran businessman who knew what he was doing—we were attacked by so-called ex-government officials who held themselves out as income tax officers and were looking for 'extra services' in return for 'maintaining peace in our office'. The alternative we were threateningly informed was boundless and bottomless enquiries, that is, investigations without an end in sight.

By the time I managed to turn them away, another bunch of tax-inspectors invaded our already full-to-the-brim office! They were also looking for their pound of flesh irrespective of the fact whether we had any non-compliance to our name or not. On top of all this, they wanted to see the trade licence, professional tax registration, sales tax registration, labour law compliances, etc. etc. etc. irrespective of the fact, whether the same was applicable or not in our case. They were not very pleased when I, instead of taking the hint and offering them their 'legally mandated hafta' kept digging and searching for the required licences in the never-ending list of licences that a business in India must have.

Finally they told me an amount of money that would help them stop trying to think of any more obscure licences required by law and leave.

I was exhausted. An entire working day had been wasted trying to appease legal extortionists instead of doing meaningful and productive work.

Dear reader, I quit.

3

ON MY OWN

I started practising as an independent chartered accountant.

For a new chartered accountant trying to practice on his own, the world was a very tough place and clients very difficult to come by. However, I created a niche by offering my clients a comprehensive range of services with integrated solutions covering taxation, company law and allied matters. There were very few chartered accountants at the time who focused on company law and my education and background helped me to establish myself in this area conveniently.

An anecdote that has invaded my mind while reminiscing about my CA days is very funny. With company law as my main focus, I had to visit the tax department once or twice each week, but I tried to keep my visits short and as few as possible, thus restricting myself in dealing in the most select cases. In those days tax officials had a peculiar habit of calling all their assessees at the same time, around 11 in the morning and then kept all of us waiting until 4 or 5 p.m. for our turn with the officer. Having waited one full day without bread and water, the next day I decided to turn up simply at 4:30, which was met with a big frown from the ITO who was not happy with me not showing up at 11 a.m. as mentioned in the notice. I retorted that being a professional I have a lot on my plate and can't waste my whole day waiting outside his chamber. He was equally adamant of his right to make me wait an entire working day before he granted me an audience.

A long verbal duel ensued. Voices were raised; screams were heard. The entire department stopped by to gawk at this young boy arguing with the taxman. In the end, surprisingly he accepted my point of view and gave me a promise to never keep me waiting in the future. I was ecstatic. It seemed that I had single-handedly demolished the Berlin Wall (a historical event that had happened very close to this personal victory).

The equation of my time versus the amount of banknotes that I am prepared to shell out—0 if you are curious by the way—is so embedded in our system that today it has released itself from the confines of a stuffy government office and leaped onto all forms of societal conduct. It is not that all government officers and inspectors are corrupt, neither is corruption confined to austere government offices. Corruption depends on a nature susceptible to bullying and zero confidence in one's own abilities to make money. Our present system simply does not have the required measures to catch, punish and deter these pitiful bullies.

Let me tell you another anecdote to explain—one day, one of my father's acquaintances asked me to deposit his cheque for the tax amount and submit his tax-returns which he had prepared on his own. When I looked over the documents, I realized that he had not claimed a lot of allowable deductions. And so, I got to work—by applying my knowledge and understanding of the company law I succeeded in reducing his tax payable amount by almost ₹25 lacs! And so, along with his much-reduced tax-returns, I of course handed him the bill for my professional services amounting to ₹5,000. He took my hard work and ignored my bill saying, 'Will you really take money from your old uncle?'

As all corruption does, this incident too ignited within me deep frustration, but I also realized that while tax-planning I am actually helping the corrupt evade taxes because of bad laws, thus causing economic and social loss to India, without adding any value to the society. Not something that I had envisioned for myself. And so, although I enjoyed my work as a CA very much, despite irascible taxmen and bullying uncles, I diversified to merchant banking. It was the year 1994. The reforms in 1991-92 led to the birth of a new India, with new paradigms being worked out. The CCI (Controller of Capital Issues) was shunted out. The SEBI was born as the saviour of investors. The public issue and listing guidelines were going through a revolution of their own and the public was hungry for more. Against this backdrop, with my knowledge of company law stepping into merchant banking was the natural next step for me. The name of the company I floated for the purpose was self-explanatory—Fast Capital Growth Limited.

I successfully acted as advisor to a few public issues; all of which did quite well and provided very good returns to investors post listing. My stress was on quality issues and I never compromised. But as all things must, my fruitful days as a merchant banker came to an end, albeit prematurely. And would you believe it, corruption had a hand in this too.

1996 was a watershed year. The industry was in a good place, but merchant banking and public issues came to be haunted and hunted because of the infamous MS Shoes scandal. With the new issue market in the death throes of MS Shoes, I started dealing on the NSE, but only for a short while because unknown to me a much larger whale was waiting in the wings to grasp me.

4

LOVE STORY BEGINS

Gujarat NRE Coke Limited forced herself on me. She had run into a huge amount of debt, was discredited by the banks, had acquired a bad reputation and was basically a bad investment. But my, and my young family's life hung between the x and y axis of NRE's balance sheet. You see, Gujarat NRE was my 'family business'—the one that my father had tried to cushion me from.

Initially it was just a small trading company that my father managed and did not consider growing. But my sister's husband and son came from a Dhanbad based coal-coke background, and my father gave them NRE's support to try and build a lucrative production company from it. I think his prescience did not extend to his son-in-law's actions. Instead of using the capital bought and guaranteed on my father's and my name for NRE's interests, my sister and her family started buying properties in their own name, even stooping to forging my father's and my signatures—basically instead of using NRE's capital on NRE, they started to make themselves rich. The result was that Gujarat NRE quickly started to drain out of cash. They even created competition for NRE, from NRE's money. I was horrified.

I eschew corruption. I loathe it for the very simple reason that it reverses growth and happiness. It sucks the air out of happy relationships and leaves the people involved—one party frustrated, the other guilty. To witness it in my own house, and within those that I had loved and admired left me raw. But I could not sit around feeling depressed or distraught that I had been KO'd without even knowing that I was participating in a fight. But the boxing ring came into sharp HD quality vision in March '97, and I geared up for the fight. My extended family seemed to have suffered an earthquake and divided themselves into camps—mine and theirs. Thankfully, my father, my wife and our young family, and my in-laws stood firm—with me. I had always appreciated my luck at finding and marrying the most intelligent and compassionate woman—we both have been able to bring out the best in each other, but the strength and wisdom of my wife added to my own knowledge and deep interest in company law remain my toughest boxing gloves.

Legal battles, dirty tricks (for example, a letter circulated to the shareholders of Gujarat NRE, stating that I would gift each folio with a gold watch), shocking threats, crank calls to my small and pre-teen children, and even a Bond movies style car chase enlivened my experiences and my life story, but it also brought the reality of my sister and her family home to me. I realized that corruption and dishonesty could hide behind pleasant and beloved faces too.

Along with the legal war, with the side-dish of deplorable actions meant to harm me and my family, I also had to breathe new life into a much abused and ravished Gujarat NRE. With zero knowledge of coal, coke or metallurgy and a previous disinterest in owning my own business, I took the challenge of fighting for my future happiness and financial security.

With the occasional ₹200 in my pocket and my trusted safari suit, I learnt the ropes on the job. On the other side of the country, NRE's operations in faraway Gujarat tested my mettle and endurance. But with patience and genuine intent I asked for help from my bankers. It took some time because the father-son duo with their brash and corrupt dealings had soured and salted NRE's relationship with them, but eventually my straightforward and honest approach created trust.

And as all things do—Gujarat NRE's troubles too came to an end, giving rise to a happy and profitable company. 5+ years of blood, sweat and integrity at last paid off. Gujarat NRE in the year 2003-4 was a respected, rich, AA—credit company with a bright future.

And despite all efforts by myself, duly aided by my father to the contrary, I became an industrialist.

5

WHOLE NEW WORLD

In 2004, I received an offer to buy a coal mine in Australia. The mine was in the Illawarra region on the South Coast of New South Wales, famous for its excellent prime coking coal. Gujarat NRE had been a happy customer in the past. I snapped it up immediately. It was a historical mine—the oldest coal mine in Australia, with 20+ years of coal left to be mined but facing permanent closure, set amidst the lush and beautiful city of Wollongong.

I am the very first Indian to control and manage a publicly listed company and mines in Australia. As such I had no precedent in how to manage a coal mine in Australia. As with Gujarat NRE in India, Gujarat NRE in Australia too began with me rolling up my sleeves and learning the ropes on the job.

The intricacies of running a coal mine, of approvals needed from the local and federal governments, of building a strong relationship between the company and the local community, of working in an office setup which did not have peons—who would ask me whether I wanted to eat jhal muri or ghughni every hour and carry my bags for me. In fact, my new office that sat on a lush hill with its innards full of coal was nowhere near to any food joint! One of the first things that I noticed in my new office was a sign over the sink in the pantry that proclaimed, 'Your mother does not work here! Wash your own dishes!'

Along with learning to understand the running of a mine, I had to learn to understand the culture of the people in this new country. It was a completely new world. Exciting and exhilarating.

The Aussies were as enamoured by my 'Indianness' and me as I was by them. They could not wrap their minds around the fact that I was a pure vegetarian. In a tv interview, one of my employees even commented that my family and I were complete vegetarians in a conspiratorial tone.

I set about discovering and understanding this new land and how I could make my business flourish.

A coal mine in Australia requires a lot of government approvals. Due to my experiences in India this was something I was dreading. In India to ask for approvals for the most necessary things for a business was akin to climbing Mount Everest without any gear. But when I stepped out to ask for the required approvals, I found to my pleasant shock that I did not need to push against any wall. The government itself invited me, asked me my requirements, performed due diligence and gave the required approvals without even hinting at a single cent of money. It really was a whole new world. For the first time I was not made to feel like a smuggler or a criminal, but like a respected businessman who could run his business with his integrity and conscience intact. It made work that much more enjoyable and attractive. I dove in head first at the coalface.

The new longwall mining equipment acquired by Gujarat NRE, on display prior to its installation at NRE No. 1 Colliery.

The wonderfully corruption-free and responsive business, political and social environment of Australia induced me to give back tenfold to the community and country that had adopted me as their own. I looked around trying to ascertain how could I return the love and acceptance that I had received. But here too, Australia differed from India. The local community did not need me to build them schools or toilets or streetlights. The democratic government, by efficiently utilizing the taxes received took care of all the basic necessities of roti, kapda and makaan. People needed money for the further development of self, and society.

The very first charity that I chose to support was the Light and Hope Clubhouse. It is a charity working towards bettering the health of people suffering from mental illnesses. They were just starting out when they came to me and did not even have a building that they could house their patients in.

The first meeting of the Committee of the Light and Hope Foundation that I attended was held in one of the City Council rooms. The room was full of people enthusiastic about the cause that they had come together for, animatedly talking about the course of action needed and how they could resolve the problems before them.

Sitting amongst them was the then Lord Mayor of Wollongong. But there was no way that I could have identified him. There were no security milling about him, no secretaries demanding his attention and no people giving him any kind of recognition.

In India, such a meeting if at all attended by a governing mayor of the city would have been full of speeches given by the mayor and the real work would have started after he or she had left. In Wollongong, the mayor was not given any precedence or occasion for a speech. He was simply there because he too wanted to make a difference and was eager to actively work towards that change.

This negation of VIP culture was astounding and refreshing. Nobody needed their butts licked; nor were there people who wanted to get ahead by licking butts. People just wanted an honest smile and a simple handshake to start working, and as long as it was within the realms of the law, no other favours were demanded or expected. It was mind-bending. I committed a voluntary social royalty of 5 cents for every ton of coal shipped out of Russelvale colliery, which I of course honoured.

The next cry for help that came my way has become the stuff of legends.

One afternoon two men walked into my office at Russelvale. One of them was tall like most Aussies looked to me, and balding and bearded. The other was also tall, but taller than most Aussies looked to me. He had bright blue eyes and blonde hair. Both looked extremely dejected. I had no idea who they were, except that they had taken an appointment to meet and talk to me about a local basketball club called the Hawks.

Handling two different businesses in two different continents did not leave me with a lot of leisure time on my hands. So I had heard and read in passing about a local sports club's efforts to save itself from going under, but did not really know the specifics. The two men now standing in my office were Wayne Morris, the then CEO of Wollongong Hawks and Mat Campbell the then captain, and the face of 'Save the Hawks campaign'.

Mat and Wayne explained the plight of the historical community club. The Hawks had belonged to the community of Wollongong since the 1970s. But now new rules in the National Basketball League demanded that they produce a bank guarantee of AU$ 1 million to prove their liquidity or they would be shut down. They just needed somebody to stand by them and vouch for them with money. I wanted to think over the matter before making a decision, but I saw the pain in their eyes that I had personally gone through in 1996-97. They just needed somebody to stand by them. I said—Yep!

Their eyes widened with disbelief, then they blinked, and Wayne said, 'Excuse me, but if you are sure of your decision I will have to call them right now and confirm that. 3 p.m. is when they make the decision.' The clock showed 2:30 p.m. They had given up hope. I was their last-ditch effort that they probably did not expect to work out.

And thus my fascination and love for basketball began.

My relationship with the Hawks was truly symbiotic, proving one good turn deserves another. In exchange for my hand of financial guarantee, the Hawks invited me into the local community. Locals started to come up to me to have a chat, to thank me for saving their Saturday evening entertainment, and to give me tips on basketball. It was warm and exciting. I belonged to the community now.

In 2009, the local paper announced me to be the 'Mercury person of the Year' and there were whispers that I should be running for the upcoming mayoral elections! The former was humbling and gratifying; the latter in the beginning was shocking and then laughter inducing. I have no interest in politics!

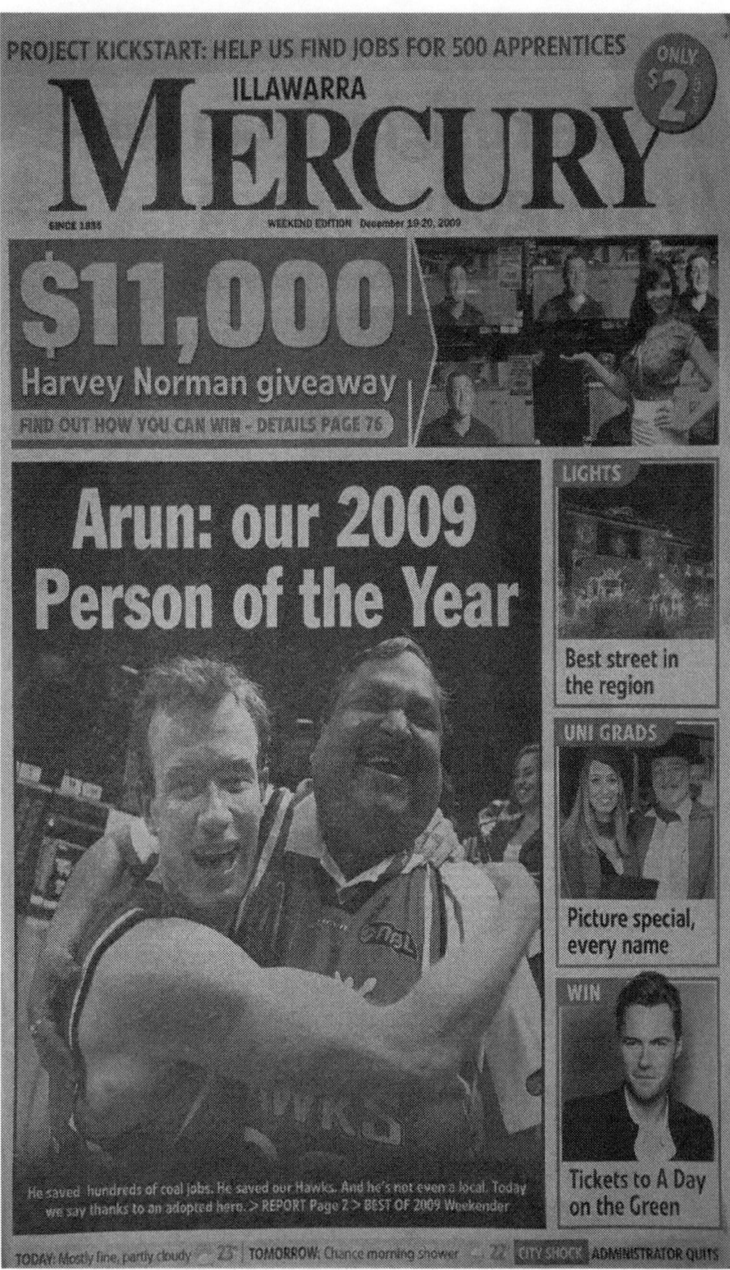

Courtesy: Illawarra Mercury

Arun Jagatramka

SAVING THE WOLLONGONG HAWKS basketball team was a snap decision for Arun Jagatramka, but it fitted perfectly with his business philosophy.

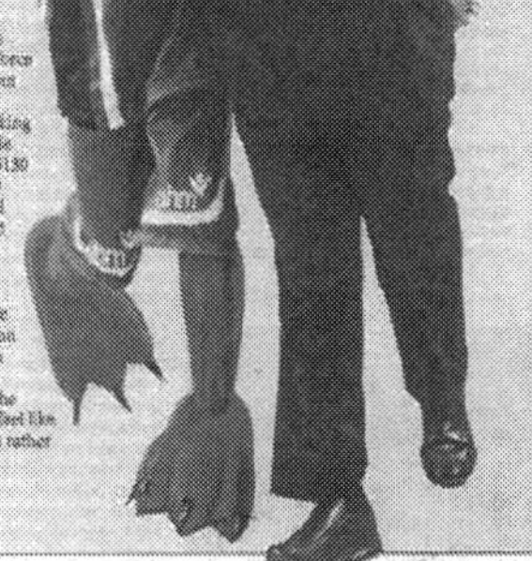

Business: Phil Shoard and the blast furnace workers

The reline of No 5 Blast Furnace at the Bluescope steelworks in Port Kembla was by far the biggest vote of confidence in the Illawarra by any corporation this year.

Courtesy: Illawarra Mercury

The most shocking experience that Australia has given me is my encounters with the Aussie Income Tax department. The Australian income tax officer called ATO, in writing gives a date and time that they would like to visit our premises, gives a very good reason for the intent of this visit, and asks if the recommended date and time is okay by us.

On the appointed date and time tax officials knock on the metaphorical door, sit in the appointed small cabin offered to them and very *very* courteously ask for only those documents that they have come to see. I emphasize, ASK for the documents that they want to see. If you are not informed you will not even know or realize that the people from the Tax department are in residence. Everybody can walk in and out of the office as any usual day.

Compare this to our experiences in India. The Income Tax department in India works in only one way. It RAIDS. The office is, for all intents and purposes assigned a yellow 'Crime Scene—Do Not Enter' tape, where the entire day's working is put to a screeching halt, and the entire office and all its employees are made to run circles around the taxmen.

You have a flight to catch, which you had booked because of course the Tax department did not inform you of its intended arrival? Forget it. Whatever work or leisure opportunity you had scheduled is ground down to cinders. You had scheduled a half-day visit to your mother recuperating in the hospital? Poor you, and your poor mother. The Indian Tax department could not care less. At the least you could call up and tell her you are unable to visit and ask after her health. Umm ...What? No outside communication allowed.

You stand, preferably bent at the waist, while the taxmen rip apart your office looking for that one document that will enable them to ask for the fine and overhead kharcha-paani from you.

I started to regale people with a self-learned truth—India has law, China has order, and Australia has both—Law and Order. The difference, and the impact of Rule of Law as opposed to Rule of Men came as a real eye-opener to me while in Australia. Suddenly I understood the true meaning of living in a Free Country, without feeling ostracized and enslaved by the powers that be.

Another trust building practice that I experienced there was that, Australia does not tolerate blackmail. One's past actions do not have any bearing on present decisions. Legal cases resolved in the past do not become fodder for future extortion attempts by government agencies.

As a business owner in Australia, the differences between owning a business in India as opposed to Australia, brought out the inconveniences and corruption in India in sharp contrast.

The absolute absence of 'VIP culture' and the friendliness of the people were astounding at first, and heart-warming throughout. The acceptance that the people of a country of whom I was not even a citizen, gave me, made me realize the bitter rivalries and petty differences that plagued and defeated my India from within. The prejudices that we hold for each and every caste, religion, gender and community is what defeats us on the national and international arena.

Every Australian, despite their ethnic, cultural and economic differences is always simply first and foremost an Aussie.

I yearn for that acceptance in India and the shared identity and joy of being an Indian.

6

DHARMAADA

My father used to tell me, 'Son, a percentage of your earnings should go to dharmaada—charity. You owe this to the society that has nurtured you.' Seems logical to me. When NRE regained her credibility and started earning enough I looked around for the charities and social needs that I could help out with. There were many initiatives which I found worth supporting. CSR (corporate social responsibility) as it is termed today, has been the bedrock of my professional ethics from the very beginning of my business endeavours. NRE and I started getting involved in various ways, from schools and educational institutes to street-lights, and from hospitals to local health, hygiene and sanitation.

However, a question that has bothered me is, whether CSR (corporate social responsibility) all about money? Is it just about allocating some funds for some social welfare project? Where is my personal commitment and involvement? Is it not my duty to contribute to the greater cause of nation building than just spending on some community project because it is a requirement by law? While Gujarat NRE and I continued with the conventional CSR, I undertook the greater cause of contributing to nation building within my limited capacity as my mission.

Due to my own experiences, I wanted to address the all-pervasive corruption and the apathy attached to it, which made the idea of an honest Indian businessman, a fantastic dream. I want to be an honest Indian Businessman.

But at that time, nobody could imagine even talking about the bribes that they had to give to get the most basic and fundamental jobs accomplished. It was an accepted evil that nobody wanted to point out.

I decided, if the elders are too afraid to talk, let's talk to the children. What kind of a country would they want to inherit? What kinds of businesses would they like to run?

The year 2009 was an iconic year. Gujarat NRE and thus I, got the opportunity to jumpstart my dream of fighting corruption in India.

The daughter of one of my wife's friends was a student at Nirma University, one of the premier technological institutes in Gujarat. She was the president of the student committee of that year, and was looking for sponsors to fund their annual science and technology festival. When she approached me, I saw before myself the rare chance to interact with the Future of India. If I played this right, through this festival I would get to meet and interact with the people who would inherit India.

She, intelligent girl, got her entire team together and the very first Gujarat NRE Integrity Theme Presentation Contest was born.

We decided on two topics, the first—'India of My Dreams'. Through this I wanted to know what dreams did the new generation see for their country, for my India. Were they similar to what I had seen in my youth? Did they have any plans and ideas that they thought would create positive change? Would they succeed, where we had failed?

The second topic was, 'No bribes, no illegal moves, no out of the way favours—can we pledge?'

Dear reader, it was such a success.

The huge auditorium was filled to the brim and humming with excitement. The entries were intelligent, thought-provoking and practical. They filled me with pride and hope for my nation's future.

The youth expressed their hopes and vision of a developed, strong and a corruption-free India. They pledged to be the torchbearers of the nation where there would be no bribes, no illegal moves and no out-of-the way favours, and where merit is the norm and transparency would be the name of the game. It was a charged-up atmosphere where the future of the nation poured out their belief and exhibited their strong resolution to shape the country on the principles of the founding men and women of our nation.

In the same year, perhaps impressed by the success of Gujarat NRE @ I-Fest 2009 and equally frustrated with the system of things in India, IIM Ahmedabad invited us to present a contest targeting corruption for their annual Insight 2009. We decided on the topic—'Does Corruption Feed Terrorism? How Can We get Rid of Such Corruption?'

The ball was in motion now!

7

THE BOXING RING IS CONSTRUCTED

2008 was a devastating year for the world financial economy. But we, in India were not immediately affected by it. However, trickling down through the years leading up to the Mumbai terror attack on 26 November 2008, a continuous series of bombs and terror attacks had splattered and harangued India. The attack on Mumbai was just the final nail in the coffin. The nexus between Corruption in India and Terrorist Acts against India became as clear as day.

We realized that the bombings and the attacks were possible because the small bribes that the common Indian paid to navigate through life was funding the guns that the terrorists aimed at us! It was street level corruption that disrupted the fabric of life in the country.

It was time to end this assault on our lives.

Since 2004, I have been organizing a premier conference on steel and its raw materials every alternate year. Top industrialists, policymakers and thinkers in the world of steel, its raw materials and associated businesses grace the Global Steel Conference, creating a heady mix of ideas, action and change.

In January 2009, I introduced the Integrity Chapter to the Global Steel Conference. Corruption and the various ways in which it was hampering and stopping progress and development in India needed to be addressed. I had have had enough of people, especially us industrialists pushing this thorn under the carpet, but treading on it and getting pricked again and again.

I wanted us to start talking about the pervasive Corruption that we have to deal with every day and to generate ideas and find solutions to this demon.

The response was immense. Policymakers, legal eagles, businesspersons, CID chiefs, even one Mr Arvind Kejriwal, then not so well known, used Global Steel's platform to voice their frustrations against corruption and their ideas and ways that we could demolish it. Eminent social reformers—Dr J.J. Irani, Tata Sons; Mr Amar Pratap Singh, Director-CBI; Mr Sanjaya Baru, Editor-Business Standard; Mr Vikram Chandra, NDTV; eminent jurists Mr Harish Salve and Mr P.P. Rao; Mr T.S.R. Subramanian, former Cabinet secretary; Dr P.P. Sangal; Ms Madhu Kishwar; eminent advocate Mr K.T.S. Tulsi; Mr Prakash Singh, former police chief—had Global Steel's delegates interested in the work that they had already put into their specific fields and what more was needed to be done and how they thought these much needed reforms could be brought about.

Through peaceful dialogue and an honest exchange of ideas, the conversation that always tip-toed and seemed to walk around the problem of corruption was brought into sharp focus and put a target over Corruption in India, marking it for imminent defeat.

Mission accomplished.

April 2011 suddenly saw a national uprising against corruption on a scale previously unthought-of. Till then, for two years I had been struggling to put corruption, and our need to fight against it in the mainstream, and suddenly I discovered that it was the mainstream. And so one fine day, to my utter and delighted bewilderment, I awoke to discover that I had reached my goal, which even a couple of months back people cautioned me would take me ten years to reach!

But wait, the fight is still not over. Corruption has been identified as a disease pricking our economic and social growth, but it still has not been conquered.

Having won the first victory in typical Indian style—with Ahimsa, I decided to jump straight into the next stage of the operation. I started to identify the various maladies associated with corruption, and formulate ways to weed out corruption prevalent in our society. To that end, I started to organize conferences on specific topics like Black Money, RTI (Right to Information), Police Reforms, Corporate Governance, and Governance in Public & Private Sectors. At the same time continuing to engage with the youth through contests with topics such as Enforced Compliance, Questioning the Trust Deficit in the country, etc.

What was exhilarating was that these topics and issues had started to make their way into the mainstream media, albeit with a two-year delay, but it gave me the confidence that my voice was being heard.

8

DUGUNA LAGAAN DENA PADEGA!

A few years ago, the media was agog and salivating at the 'news' when tax officers raided a famous Bollywood actress's—one of the highest tax payers of the country—house at 7 in the morning and they found another actor also there. The gossip mills churned excitedly about this 'sensational breaking news'.

NOT ONE PERSON thought to enquire WHAT WAS THE Income Tax Department doing at an Indian citizen's house at 7 in the morning?! Why do our enforcement agencies feel the need to treat us—the citizens of India as common criminals?

Our erstwhile colonial masters largely, for obvious reason, were uninterested in the development—of either Indians or India. Their officers therefore conducted themselves accordingly, extracting with a deliberate intent and view to weaken and enslave—similar to extortionists. The revenue thus collected by sucking even the last drop of blood from every Indian was used to line the pockets of the entire hierarchy of the British civil servants posted in India, and still the leftover sent back to their own country to be utilized in its own development.

Why—

- 72 years after gaining independence;
- 72 years of self-rule; and
- 72 years of Indian civil servants born and educated in India

are we still treating ourselves like enslaved and colonized people???

Why do the Indians working for the Indian government still behave and conduct themselves like colonial masters? Which country other than India, are they serving? And instead of lining British officers' pockets, now our hard-earned rupees is being extorted to fill the pillow covers, and the mattresses of those 'lucky' enough to be in positions of governmental power.

I know, this last paragraph will enrage and hurt a lot of Indians—both honest, and peculiarly dishonest.

But I am not writing this book to accuse or malign anybody. We, as a nation are still unable to destroy the shadow of destructive imperialism— which has resulted in us still being a 'developing economy'.

Let me share a few personal experiences to illustrate—

1. TAX TERRORISM

Instead of a transparent system of—processing taxes, helping the citizens to file our tax-returns easily and conveniently, ensuring that the taxes collected are utilized in the correct governmental departments (education, police, etc.), and investigating the few inevitable black sheep that seem to not understand the return value of taxes on our own social lives, the Indian Income Tax Department works as if their boss is none other than Gabbar Singh!

With archaic 'tax-targets' income tax officers are dispatched to perform the obsolete practice of going around all the corporate offices with a view to 'collect'. Since 'tax collection' based on 'tax targets' is the sole goal of these 'tax officers', and our frustratingly opaque system is yet to build any accountability for our government officials—bullies and goondas thrive.

Everybody dealing with them knows exactly who these are, but in the complete absence of an ombudsman, a robust complaints department, and the bad policies that rule our lives, these dacoits are rewarded with promotions, instead of being punished for their unconstitutional actions.

The presently incumbent Modi government has opened the door to a better future by compulsorily retiring a few of these corrupt officers, but even a government with such an immense democratic mandate is unable to actually punish and hold our government officers/bureaucracy accountable for their actions.

So one of my many, many experiences (like every Indian navigating life in India), with one such specimen that I wanted to relate here is an anecdote from 2009, when the effects of the Great Recession of 2008 was in full swing, and on a global scale every industry, business, and work was suffering.

An officer in the local Income Tax Department had made a name for himself—not for being an officer—but for being the biggest goonda.

He constantly maligned the Income Tax Department by misusing the monopolistic powers awarded to him by systematically taking away the rights that we hold, both as an Indian citizen and a human being.

He had a habit of barging into any and every place that he desired as if he had paid for it by his own hard earned rupees, because our system does not require our government officers to seek for a convenient time, or provide notice of their intended arrival, or work with us in any shape or form, he considered himself above all rules and laws. Consequently, he accompanied by his gang of taxmen used to barge in the chosen victim's office demanding immediate attention from everybody at the cost of our work, putting an imaginary, but very much enforced yellow do not cross tape around the office, destroying the entire working day, refusing to leave until their atrocious demands—of over the table and under the table payments were immediately met.

One fine afternoon he got the unfortunate idea to grace our office too. Luckily for both of us, I imagine, I was in Australia on that day. As per his habit he barged in with his usual gang without notice, went around the entire office—disrupting everybody, and ensuring all work was immediately halted. Without any code of conduct and/or rules informing their behaviour he strode into my chamber too—but the stacks of books, magazines, photos, and other literature on integrity, ethics, and fighting corruption that inhabit my chamber gave him pause.

Perhaps his brain just couldn't comprehend the idea of integrity, and his feet hurried him out of my chamber, under the fear that it might infect him with ethics.

Even after going through, and disturbing the entire office, they had failed to find any document based on which they could fabricate a demand, and so he decided to extort a hefty cheque towards an illegal advance tax payment for that year (illegal because we had already paid it). Perhaps this was simply to protect his reputation of being a goonda.

He also extracted a promise from my vice-president to meet him in his office later—no reason provided. I believe my office, full of evidence of integrity and ethics was uncomfortable to him and discouraged him to demand any more cash.

When my vice-president honoured the demand for this unnatural meeting, the 'tax collector's' personal 'hafta vasooli'—a figure much, much higher than the advance tax that he had extorted from my office was communicated.

When I was informed of the figure, I sent a simple response to him—

'We don't pay bribes. Whatever problems and obstacles that a corrupt government officer creates for not giving in to his unjust and unlawful demands, will be a damage of a few percentage points from our retained profits—a loss to us, of course, but a bigger loss to our society. If an officer pursues this corrupt behaviour, it will force us as a company to file a strong complaint, and pursue it till it reaches its just end in a court of law, and probably destroy the corrupt officer's career. So the choice was his—whether to continue to extort us or forget us since there was no cash for him anyhow.' The message hit the nail on the head!

The next that I heard of that particular parasite was in early June 2019. When the incumbent government dismissed twelve senior officers for corruption, his name was included.

While obviously there was a universal feeling of justice granted in the company, there was also a sense of frustration at our system, that allowed such a bully to rise to the rank of a 'senior officer'. Moreover, even such a strong government was only able to dismiss such bullies, not punish them, for the years of torture and torment that they have given to the citizens of India.

He along with his gang transformed a healthy and vibrant working office, into a tiny police state complete with an Iron Curtain where he was the dictator. They cut-off all communication and barred everyone's natural freedom of movement (nobody was allowed to leave or enter), they demanded whichever and whatever files and documents that they could think of, and spoke to everyone as if they were talking to slaves.

Even though I was in an entirely different continent with a widely different time zone, as the promoter, and an entrepreneur—I have to keep all my operations, offices working smoothly, and thankfully our 21st century is well equipped for smooth and efficient communication.

But on that particular day, a gang of government officers misusing their monopolistic powers had taken away all natural freedoms and nullified the ease and convenience provided by the 21st century, thus digressing to the anxious and inconvenient days of old and my technologically efficient office was forced to go into radio silence. At the end of a completely wasted working day, when the legally mandated terror was finally 'handled', and shooed away, my staff were able to inform me of the horrendous visit.

Wouldn't it be better, and more beneficial to everybody if the Income Tax Department, and all government departments for that matter, instead of behaving like goondas and colonial masters uninterested in the welfare of the citizens of the country that they profess, and are supposed to serve, are able to actually perform their duties without resorting to behaving like bullies and torturing their own people? How can we possibly achieve this beautiful goal?

Let's try these—

1. Remove our prejudice that we are all chors!
    You might say easier said than done. But look at the Australian example—Australia was England's penal colony! By its very definition it was a land of criminal exile. But shucking off their agonizing past, the Aussies reformed their government systems to be transparent and full of trust. And that has resulted in a Trust based polity, complete with a happy and successful citizenry.

2. Put a strict 3-year limitation on initiating any enquiry or investigation by any agency under any law.

    'Then how shall we catch and punish those criminals who have wronged us?' you might wonder. अब पछताए क्या होत, जब चिड़िया चुग गयी खेत? Thankfully for my editor there is also a perfect English equivalent to this idiom—Working on age-old files with no end in sight is equal to *closing the stable door after the horse has bolted*. Instead of actually catching the criminals, it creates blackmail fodder and corruption avenues for government officers looking to misuse their monopolistic and discretionary powers.

3. There needs to be a practical and conducive exchange of real-world data between citizens and government officers to achieve an honest tax submission, and consequent use of that tax for our own development.

4. The onus must always reside with the government officer to justify the need to interact with a citizen.

5. An Indian citizen's right to dignity must always be respected. When there is a justifiable reason for any government agency to enquire and/or investigate any action, notice must be given for the proposed visit, the visit must not take away the human right to dignity and freedom of movement

of anyone present—any and all interviews must be time-bound.

6. All enquiries and/or investigations must be concluded within twelve months from the date of initiation. In the rarest of rare case ample proof must be provided to continue by the team of investigating officers.

2. TAX TARGETS BLIND TO ACTUAL INCOMES

2004 had been a bumper year for the industry. Gujarat NRE had clocked super profits—*Business Standard* had labelled us 'Supermodel of the Year'. We had achieved the first rank on all parameters—a Super Rank! For a company that had been struggling to survive a mere five years ago, this was ground-breaking. The tax-amount that we had paid for 2004 exceeded more than 800 times than that of the tax paid in 1999!

But as I have said innumerable times, incomes fluctuate. Factors such as the global industry, the domestic industry, the market, the political climate, etc., significantly influence the fate of a business. And our coke market in particular—aptly symbolizing the product that it trades in—is extremely volatile.

So after a super bumper 2004, the year 2005 although profitable looked like a loss on the graph, when compared to the previous year.

Obviously without the same amount of profit as the previous year, the amount of tax paid was comparatively lower. But our oblivious Income Tax Department kept chasing us to demand an even higher tax payment than last year!

One of the senior–most tax officers in the Investigation Wing demanded that I personally pay him a visit.

His opening remark as I entered his office was, 'You are receiving a lot of limelight these days!'

I smiled and said, 'Sir, if a ₹5-lac tax paying company pays ₹43 crores within 5 years, I think the limelight is justified.'

'That's ok, that's ok, but I need tax for this year too, and it has to be higher than last year!' the taxman replied. 'We can't allow the tax collection to fall down. We have Targets, and we must collect at least 10-20 per cent more than last year!'

He continued. 'And if a big assessee like you pays less it won't do. You have to pay more. We have to meet our target!'

This came as a Super Shock to me. As an Indian citizen, I have an extremely vague idea, and absolutely no say in the 'tax targets' that are set by the Income Tax Department each quarter. As a tax-paying entity in a democracy it is fantastic that I am not even included in the conversation for this archaic practice of 'tax-targets' that we compel ourselves to go through each financial quarter.

Consequently, the result is that instead of 'tax targets' being based on my capability of paying tax for each quarter, it is based on a rough 10 per cent increase from that paid in the previous quarter, regardless of income and profits earned! Is it any wonder that a large number of tax-paying entities in our country feel compelled to hoard cash to guard against the income fluctuations, that our policy makers and the tax department for some strange reason turn a completely blind eye to?

I said, 'I believe that the tax we pay is based on the income we earn, and there cannot be any target on incomes as incomes fluctuate. We have paid our taxes according to our income. Last year, through a wonderful melange of our hard work and favourable external factors we earned super-profits. Accordingly, we could give back to society with a super tax. This year the market was not favourable, but because we are carrying a large inventory from the previous year, we could still finish off this quarter with a reasonable profit, as opposed to none at all. Basically, when society helps industry profit, only then can industry give back to society. Consequently the expected advance tax is being paid on time, there really is no need for you to worry.'

Further super shocking answers awaited me. I still have a hard time believing that an actual officer of the Income Tax Department of the Government of India said the following words to me—

'No, no, no! *You should not have paid so much tax last year!* Who asked you to? Because that is why we are having a problem. Your unusually large tax payment's credit has been taken by my predecessor. And this year, I will be cutting a sorry figure because of you! My "collection" will go down because of you!'

I mean—I am the one paying the tax, and the 'tax collector' is getting credit for my hard work? And on top of it, I am being accused by his successor of performing my civic duties honestly?!

Why does the Indian tax officer's performance depend on how much tax they can extort from the citizens of India, instead of their own work ethic, and own honest hard work? Instead of 'tax collectors' and the bane of the common Indian, why can't we reform our Income Tax Department to be made up of tax processors—who are able to process the taxes submitted, ensure that the money is being utilized in the required sections and chase the few exceptions who do not understand the value of tax consciously invested in our own society, without ravaging the dignity of everyone involved, the tax officer included?

I replied, 'Sir, you may go by your inscrutable, and mysterious targets, but we have no choice but to go by our business earnings. I cannot produce money from thin air, and I refuse to indulge in any illegal actions and the black market just to satisfy your misguided targets. I have paid tax when I earned a profit, and will continue to do so, whenever the society and consequently the market helps me earn a profit.

If you are looking for a regular 10-20 per cent increase periodically, regardless of industry and market conditions, then consider last year's payment as OTS (one time settlement) from Gujarat NRE, and me.'

Bulging eyes regarded me with surprise—'What?!'

I explained further, 'Yes, Sir. Based on tax of ₹5 lacs that we had paid in the year 2000, if you increase that by 10 per cent every year, and calculate for the rest of my professional life—let's say next eighty years—the total will still be less than the amount that I have paid in 2004–5.

'If that pleases you, you may consider full and complete OTS paid for the next eight decades, and Gujarat NRE is tax exempt from now on.'

A mad stare was the only reply I got this time.

The awkward meeting finally ended with a muttered, 'What nonsense.'

But thankfully, the message seemed to have been driven home. I did not hear from the tax department for the next couple of years—during which I of course filed my taxes regularly, since he had not seemed too keen on the OTS proposal.

How can we achieve the dream of becoming a rich and developed country? Let's try these—

1. Transform our government machinery and systems to become more transparent.
2. Use data analysis and data management to determine what the tax for a given period of time for every entity should be.

3. Instead of incentivising poverty incentivise wealth. The present government has taken a small step in this direction with the Jan Dhan Yojana.

4. Hold our bureaucracy accountable for their actions. The performance of all government officers must depend on their own work ethic and honest hard work instead of how much power they exert over the citizenry.

5. A robust ombudsman to be introduced in all government machinery.

6. Harness the technology of Blockchain. Each taxpayer using her/his unique key will be able to see the breakdown of where our tax rupees is being utilized—police, education, infrastructure, transport, health, arts, research, etc. Because of the immutability of blockchain, any leakages enroute will be immediately identified, and addressed. Thus ensuring Certainty of Punishment. When we Indians begin to see and experience the benefits of our hard-earned rupees actually being utilised in public facilities that make our day-to-day lives easier, safer and more convenient—taxes will be filed honestly, and regularly.

7. Our government urgently needs to reform and build Trust into our systems.

3. NO FUNDAMENTAL RIGHT TO LIBERTY!

'You are hereby required personally to attend my office on _____ date at _____time. You are not to depart until you receive my permission to do so.'

!!!

Traditionally the coke industry had been exempted from excise. We were subject to a simple sales tax which we of course paid honestly. In 2011, excise duty in the form of central value added tax (CENVAT) was suddenly introduced.

Since we have to import our entire stock of raw material—as coking coal is one of the few things that India does not have naturally—which we then convert to coke, and then sell it, the countervailing duty (CVD) that we pay on imports is fully CENVAT-able with the excise duty that is to be paid on sale of our final product, that is, coke. As such, we always enjoyed surplus credit in our excise account. Thus, we were not required to make any payments towards excise. Also, since all our sales were based on a selling price, with taxes added, the rate of excise duty was passed onto our customers allowing them to take credit for it at their end.

Suddenly in 2016, five years after the imposition of CENVAT, the excise department desired to conduct a detailed investigation for the first five years of the excise duty. Accordingly, officers of the Central Excise Department, situated near one of our plants, decided to visit us without any notice and took away our entire inventory of paperwork—MORE THAN 300-400+ files!

The pretext provided—checking the past five years of excise record.

But then, why did they need to confiscate the documents from before 2011 when CENVAT did not even exist? Perhaps they liked the extra work, or perhaps they just wanted to claim that they had confiscated such a large number of documents from a legal Indian entity to simply exert their monopolistic and discretional powers, that is not subject to any accountability. It is obviously impossible to even scan through such a large number of documents, let alone derive any meaning or evidence of wrongdoing or honest business practice, no matter the strength of manpower deployed!

And so, after abusing their monopolistic powers of raid and confiscation without proof and zero consequent result, they moved onto the next step of their lazy and dictatorial process—summoning the plant accountant to record a statement.

Honouring the summons, our accountant went to their office at 2 in the afternoon on the appointed day. WE DID NOT HEAR FROM HIM UNTIL 7 THE NEXT MORNING! His mobile phone had been confiscated as soon as he had entered, cutting him off from any and all communication. How is it—Why is it that in our democracy a citizen of the country who is not even a suspect for any wrongdoing, against whom the authorities have no proof of any wrongdoing can be held against our wish in direct defiance of the Constitution of India, with none of the officers held accountable???

Our accountant who had reached the Excise Department at 2 p.m. was made to wait, without any reason offered till 7 in the evening—no refreshments offered. After wasting half a day of a productive and wealth-creating Indian, a team of officers finally graced him with an audience.

The questions, and the manner in which they were asked compel us to question the enormous sacrifices that our parents, grand parents, and great grandparents suffered to give us an independent India where we will supposedly not be discriminated against or exploited.

Perhaps imagining themselves to be some version of a James Bond–style villain instead of performing their job of going through relevant papers that would have actually helped them to constructively conclude that we were not engaged in any corrupt or illegal activity, they proceeded to threaten our accountant towards a coercive confession!

When, despite their threatening and posturing they were unable to extract any information that would suit their needs of further destruction of their duties as officers of our government, our accountant was sentenced to a further untold number of waiting hours. No food or water provided or offered still, if you are curious by the way.

And still no communication allowed! I am sure you can imagine our horror, confusion and tension at the absolute radio silence and zero communication when a person who had entered a government office at 2 in the afternoon had not contacted anybody till 7 the next morning! How, how can our own government allow this to happen? How can WE the citizens boasting to be the largest democracy on this planet allow our government bodies to mistreat and exploit us in this manner???

At midnight (!) the officers again attempted to force a coercive confession, awarding another indefinite waiting period when unsuccessful.

When the Indian citizen who had done no wrong, and had no cause to be suspected, and after being held without any proof, without bread and water, finally requested REQUESTED to be released in the early hours of the morning—he was answered with a tight slap!

Next day at 7 in morning his freedom was returned to him—but at a cost still! He was ordered to return at 9:30 am for further questioning!!!

No wonder we are still a third world country. How will we develop our economy when we are not allowed to work to earn money, and the little that we are able to is squandered away by an incompetent and lazy government system.

Thankfully, when he was let go from the Excise Chamber of Horrors, his basic freedom of communication was handed back to him.

I am sure you can share my frustrated rage from that morning, when I heard the entire proceedings.

Despite being a democracy with elected members of parliament, who are supposed to represent us—the citizenry—our system has no window where we can approach, communicate, criticize and offer complaints and or suggestions to our 'representatives'.

Thankfully, technology has provided a solution, which I am sure we will be able to further refine and integrate into our democratic processes. I tagged the PMO, and the Central Board of Indirect Taxes and Customs (CBIC) on Twitter, and let them know the completely criminal conduct of the officers of the Excise Department.

Proving the strength of a transparent government machinery, the tweet had an immediate and revolutionary impact. The joint commissioner of the area called up the exploited accountant, told him not report back at 9:30, sought my number and called me. He told me that the idea was not harassment by way of an explanation.

To which I responded, 'But if you treat the employees of a legal Indian business in such a manner, how are we supposed to run efficient and wealth-creating businesses? How can you expect anybody to be compliant, when the government agencies whose job is to uphold the laws of our land fail so spectacularly?'

The phone call and the situation ended with a promise that no further harassment would be meted out, and to allow what had already been done to be foregone.

Those excise officers, as far as I know, are still incumbent, probably continuing their destructive acts against our nation, in the absence of any punishments, and still no accountability introduced.

Some very basic things that we can, and need to do to stop ourselves from getting tortured, and our human and constitutional rights revoked in our own country—

1. Orientation and training of all government officers—present, and future, needs to be focused on solving the problems brought in, and helping the citizenry instead of the present illusion of grandiose power resulting in the destructive mindset of harassment and hounding the citizens for the officers' individual and collective pounds of flesh.
2. Technology needs to be incorporated to balance out human error and prejudice.
3. A limit on the duration of time that an interviewee can be held for questioning. Dishonouring this the government officer/s become subject to prosecution.
4. Onus needs to reside with the government agency to justify any and all communication with citizens. This means—government officers actually need to work and build a strong case against a genuine wrongdoer, instead of clogging up the system with unnecessary cases and files.
5. Onus needs to be on the government officer to seek and ask for ASK FOR only those documents that they suspect will help them build a strong and robust case against a wrongdoer. Instead of the present archaic system of wasting government machinery, time, and storage space along with our hard-earned tax-rupees to confiscate any and all documents that they can get their hands on.
6. Create a Citizen's Critique system thus creating a direct channel of communication between citizens and government bodies.

4. PERSONAL GREED OVER DEVELOPMENT

Production of met coke requires two major raw materials—coking coal and water.

With Environment as our middle name, we understand and respect the need and importance of sustainable development—where industry is aware and conscious of its impact on the environment and takes strategic decisions to invest and minimize the negative effects. Thus through conscious pre-planning, and an efficient use of check dams and rainwater harvesting methods we at Gujarat NRE remove the pressure on our groundwater levels. Rather because of these conscious investments in our environment, we have been able to recharge our groundwater levels!

Gujarat NRE boasts of the most technologically advanced coke-manufacturing plants. In addition to better production, and safety protocols, consciously environment-friendly decisions are taken to reduce our carbon footprint. This has resulted in, among other things, a vibrant green belt of healthy trees and plants that surround and sustain our manufacturing plants. This in addition with the smokeless chimneys prompts the visitors to our fully operational plants to enquire with furrowed brows—'When will you begin production?', while whole tonnes of prime quality met coke is being discharged!

When one of the plants was first set up the local Industrial Development Board in its bid to attract industry had promised to supply the all essential water. But our government bodies seem to promise incentives without actually having even thought of a working plan on how to deliver these promises— leading to a huge trust deficit between the citizens and the government. And so, when even after a few years (!) had gone by without any sign of fulfilment of promises, we were left hanging to find alternate solutions.

Thankfully due to our environmentally conscious plant design, we already had invested in several rainwater harvesting tanks within the plant, but of course these were not enough to meet our industrial needs.

Within the land demarcated for industrial use that surrounds the plant, we identified a large piece of land with a large depression on one end, and a steep gradient of 60 degrees. This geographical fact has rendered that parcel of land unsuitable for any industrial development. But it is the perfect solution to our environmentally conscious water needs. We realized it would be ideal to create a rainwater harvest reservoir at this place—thus solving our water needs, while being a sustainable solution by tapping into and utilizing the abundant rains that the area receives, instead of pressuring the groundwater levels.

Moreover, instead of promoting it as a CSR project, or seeking financial support from the government, we decided to simply invest in our own future and buy the land at commercial rates with a view that the environmentally conscious and progressive source of one of our major raw materials is justified by the cost of production. We did not seek government support because that would have demanded a lot of political lobbying, which would of course translate to untoward favours and bribes—which I am never agreeable to. And till now, we as a democracy have not designed our system to eradicate political lobbying to help and aid the citizenry with innovations and enterprise. Our government machinery needs to be robust and agile to help us do our jobs with ease and convenience, as long as the task is within the confines of the law, and actually helping to create wealth for the society. And for this we need an education system that nurtures critical thinking instead of marks.

Anyway, we applied for the land—making it clear that we wanted to acquire it to develop a rain-harvesting reservoir, for our sustainable industrial needs. Sustainable industry is a new term with many still grappling with its meaning. So early in the 2000s when we proposed the idea, it was put up for clearance before the single-window committee which was headed by one of the then incumbent ministers. We were given a patient hearing—our senior executives from the plant had themselves attended the meeting to explain the then revolutionary and novel way of thinking of industry and environment sustaining each other. The minister was explained our need and aspirations towards a symbiotic relationship between industrial progress and environmental conservation. The government officers present in that meeting were impressed and did appreciate the idea very much.

But the end of the successful meeting was shattered—the incumbent minister, instead of taking a real interest in this innovative idea and having an actual conversation with us to take this idea further to develop our community, put a single condition of cash payment for his personal mattress, equal to the amount payable to the government exchequer for the land.

With a few selfish words, the fool minister—

- Doubled the price of the land;
- Completely ignored our efforts to create an environment-friendly industry;
- Completely ignored the positive effects that such a step would have had on all—the community, the industry, and the environment.
- Snatched away our dignity;
- Bared our monopolistic and opaque system that afforded him the chance to play bully—to commit the crime of extortion legally, and with no accountability.

Morally and financially we were loath to commit several wrongs in order to create something right. And so, rather than bend down to oblivious bullies, we stayed firm on the non-corrupt offer. As expected, we received their regret letter mentioning that the land had already been allotted to another party!

About a decade later that plot of land is still lying waste, if you were wondering.

This example perfectly exhibits how zero accountability, opaque meetings, and the sorry state of critical thinking in our 'political masters' has prevented real development and sustainable industry to materialize in our country.

By the way, this story does not end here—पिक्चर अभी बाकी है मेरे दोस्त!

The jilted minister like a rejected stalker used his power to put as many obstacles and irritants that his already proven petty mind could think of. For example, he repeatedly filed complaints against us to the Pollution Control Board as a result of which we were raided by the local EPC multiple times that year. Thus the ego of one person with 'power' was instrumental in wasting the time, money, and energy of two working, progress and wealth-creating entities of India.

Not once has the minister been questioned or any onus been put on his actions of disrupting the working of two legal entities—one governmental, and another industrial, repeatedly.

People like to quote great spiritual leaders with words like, 'the material is immaterial' without actually understanding the meaning behind these words.

Being a Chartered Accountant, I simply perform a cost-benefit analysis between the necessary physical and material comforts needed weighed against creating, contributing to, and living in a corrupt, and thus unhappy society. A happy and non-corrupt community will always create more wealth than a corrupt one.

How can we extract our community from this vicious quicksand of corruption?

1. Constructive criticism needs to be incorporated in our public life. Explore and harness technology to create a robust Citizen's Critique.
2. All government agencies need to be empowered to work independent of 'political masters'. Government officers must have the tools and the autonomy to make critical thinking decisions without being compulsorily influenced by elected ministers.

3. Accountability needs to be introduced in the actions of elected ministers.

4. Rule of Law must be established instead of the presently archaic system of 'rule of men'.

5. Technology needs to be introduced to enable our elected representatives to be answerable to us—the citizens of India.

6. Every minister/government body—making promises needs to provide a working plan and timeline of how these proposed promises will be achieved.

I am relating these incidents not to incriminate anyone. Because these are not one-off events that only I have suffered through. I am writing these so that We Indians may identify the frustrating lacunae in our system, and thus reform our systems to work for us, instead of the present form of against us. Our opaque and unaccountable bureaucratic system has prevented honest people from working honestly. Instead the monopolistic and discriminatory powers in the hands of a few has ensured that corrupt bullies prosper unpunished, while we as a society suffer.

5. THE LIONESS AMONGST CROCS

I am sure you have encountered many such similar experiences. One cannot exist in India without them, until we are able to reform ourselves.

But I have also encountered those Indians—citizens, government officers, and ministers—who like me desire to be honest, are capable, actually learn how to do their jobs, and thus do not even feel the need to abuse their power.

One such incident that affirmed my faith in our corruption-free future was when during one of the programs that I had participated in to continue the dialogue on and against corruption, I met an honest and capable officer of the Government of India, and it led to one of the most extraordinary events of my life.

Sometime in 2009-10 we were having a panel discussion on the CII Yi (Young Indians) platform on my favourite topic, and as usual I was very vocal about the extortionary corruption practised by the officers of the government and enforcement agencies, which of course included the Customs and Excise Department.

It so happened that the panelist sitting right next to me was the then principal chief commissioner of customs for the state of Gujarat. My remarks enraged her. I got chastised strongly—publicly and privately, against my generalized comment, 'All government officers are corrupt'.

When in a separate meeting at her office, I was able to explain my point of view with examples of my experiences as an honest industrialist navigating the corrupt hellfire of India's opaque and unaccountable system, she was also able to voice her equally frustrated experiences as an honest government officer and us seeming to being part of an utter minority. And so, my prejudiced remark of stereotyping all government officers as corrupt had obviously pained her. And I got the chance to check my prejudice.

She was so impressed by my arguments and presentations on integrity that she invited me to speak to all the customs officials in Gujarat—to make a presentation explaining the ground realities of corruption and the absolutely negative effects that such unethical practices has on not only our society but also our personal lives.

And that is how I found myself, the sole industrialist addressing a jam-packed hall full of all the customs officers from all the ports of Gujarat—commissioners, deputy-commissioners, assistant-commissioners, everyone—showing them a 20-minute long presentation on 'The Negative Effects of Corruption', and what we can do to eradicate this evil.

While the honest officers in the audience must have felt hope and strength, I am sure it would not have been a comfortable evening for the ones susceptible to corruption.

The principal chief commissioner not only declared herself to be an honest civil servant but also followed it up with action. This experience made me happy and hopeful for our better future—the honest civil servant and the honest industrialist had together created history. For that one day, we had opened a transparent dialogue between industry and government, which is still lacking today.

9

THE AWAKENING

26/11 being essentially an attack on the financial capital of India, finally pricked the business community, and forced it to sit up and take notice. Striking while the iron was hot, I initiated a select group of interested and similarly concerned people to meet and discuss on a periodic basis the day-to-day corruption that seems to flow along with other important cells in an Indian's blood, and which is one of the major factors contributing to the guns being trained on our very foreheads; without petty corruption, terrorism cannot survive; without local help facilitated by greased palms, acts of terror are impossible.

This led to the larger issue, is corruption more harmful than previously thought. Till then corruption was perceived simply as an extra financial worry, although ostensibly illegal, but a 'chalta hai' accessory.

But the realization that this chalta hai petty corruption is actually putting our hard-earned rupees directly into the pockets of those being trained to kill us, and our loved ones exposed the muck of corruption in a whole new light. The need for a concentrated effort to root out and eradicate corruption is the urgent requirement for the development and future success of our country, and put me directly on the warpath against this malice.

The year 2011 was climacteric. The passionate need for a corruption-free system resonated through the open maidans, the twisting gullies and the colonial red-bricked offices of the country. The clarion call of becoming anti-corrupt flew across the wood-panelled boardrooms, soot-filled coal mines and lush green cricket pavilions. The public demand to build and live in an honest and therefore safe society demolished dynasties and ignited the spark to drive out corruption from our lives.

The biggest challenge in the fight against corruption was the illusionary trap of perception. People did not even want to acknowledge that corruption existed, let alone that it was an evil that needed to be tackled and defeated. Corruption I found was taboo, even more so than sex or AIDS! It was the biggest pink elephant in the room that everybody fed, but none acknowledged.

Thus I had to begin by concentrating my efforts towards highlighting the need for integrity, for a corruption-free India and the evils of corruption that are eating away our roots and consequent success.

As an honest Indian businessman addressing the evil of corruption and actively engaged in eradicating it from our system since the year 2009, I am in a word, delighted. When I started my campaign for Integrity, I wondered if it would ever be successful. Whether my daydream of living without the dark shadow of corruption would ever be realized. So today, when one of the major forms of corruption—Grand or Collusive Corruption—has actually been diagnosed, accepted as a major issue of our lives and is actively being addressed, and within the space of few years since I first publicly spoke against corruption is exhilarating. But the road to Integrity demands a lot more ingredients and manual labour than what is being applied today.

10

INDIA STRUGGLING

This awareness of the pitfalls of corruption opened up a Pandora's box with a seemingly endless series of scams spilling out of its depths in quick succession. For four years between 2010 and 2014 the breaking news media increased its TRPs by lapping up the gory details of the underbelly of our rotten corrupt system, in the process virtually bringing the government to a standstill and the entire bureaucracy in a state of paralysis.

This recognition and acceptance of the severe crisis that our country was going through led to the desire for *Achhe Din*—better days. And when the BJP led by the then phenomenal chief minister of Gujarat, put forward these very words in its political campaign of 2014—the entire nation endeavoured to break the shackles of living under a corrupt system.

Breaking a thirty-year jinx of divisive coalition politics, Narendra Modi—proved that we Indians are truly united when provided with the option of an actually adept, skilled, and impartial leader who seemed to refuse to divide and suppress—with an absolute majority earned the mandate to bring the country out of its slumber, and endeavour to create a system more conducive to a happy life for the common Indian citizen.

11

ACHHE DIN

We are a young country. Although many will point out that we have a 5000-year-old history. But the future depends on our actions in the present. In 2014, India was sixty-seven years old, and still learning the ropes of governance. Various factors of caste, religion, etc. seemed to sharply divide us on frankly very weird issues. This resulted in a major portion of our population forced to live below the poverty line—deprived from the basic necessities of food, hygiene, homes. Of course this also resulted in us as a country making decisions based on our religious, and casteist beliefs, instead of the seriously important questions like—how can we create an efficient public transport system, how can we create a more justice oriented judiciary, how can we create the much needed waste management system, how can we empower our police to work for us, the citizens of India. I am sure you have more questions like these that would fill up another book.

And now, due to the pandora's box of scams, domestic industry started to flounder which led to non-payment of dues to banks, which in turn forced Indian banks to carry large NPAs on their books with no exit policy in sight.

The rot of corruption had come full circle now.

The new Modi-led government of India had the hopes of more than a billion souls pinned onto it. We want real reforms—not political gestures. And proving the strength of our democracy, our new government got right down to work. Instead of waving a short term, quickfire fairy-godmother-like wand, the Modi-led government decided to take systematic steps to root out the systematic corruption. This novel government did not discriminate along the old divisions. It seemed to work for us—the Indian citizen. Instead of the poor, it targeted poverty through schemes like the Jan

Dhan Yojana. It addressed the need for real hygiene and waste management, instead of the illusionary 'caste-purity' through the Swachh Bharat Mission. It created an affordable healthcare scheme through Ayushman Bharat. It created the Insolvency and Bankruptcy Code (IBC) to revitalize industry.

12

WHY ARE WE STILL WAITING FOR ACHHE DIN?

Despite all the cleansing efforts, we are still waiting for *Achhe Din.*

The economy has slumped further since 2017, farmers are facing a huge crisis, the middle class is frustrated, pollution levels are rising alarmingly, and the industry is being hounded.

Why?

The implementation of all the schemes, codes and missions targeted towards India's development and happiness demand much more than what is being done at present. However, these actions display our desire and drive to reform our systems to work for our happiness and success. And for that we need to address and give up our archaic prejudices that we believe divide us from within. We need to adopt Transparency, and thus create Trust within ourselves—and therefore in our system.

Even though we are suffering en masse, we are still holding on to our prejudices and privileges—the perceived differences that we believe divide us and is the very crude base of our reservation policy. Instead of truly benefitting from our diversity—which gifts us with the boon of multiple solutions to our problems, 1.3 billion perspectives and skills, of enjoying our achievements together—we regrettably focus on obsolete differences that has historically, again and again resulted in our suppression as a society.

Instead of working for the benefit of us—the Indian citizen, we focus our energies on I/me/my community/my caste/my religion/my language—so, so, so many fractured identities. The result obviously is that such proposals, if rarely, do benefit one section of our multicultural, multi-voiced society— they do inevitably hurt the other sections, which do not come under this exclusive aegis.

India has long been accused of a defunct judiciary—being one of the worst jurisdictions for enforcement of legal contracts. From the corporate law view, sick industries continued to bleed for decades without any exit policy thereby remaining a drain on the nation's resources. In 2016, in a landmark move by the government, the Insolvency & Bankruptcy Code was introduced to prevent such a long drawn legal process. While the draft code was being debated, I had a few apprehensions and critique that I shared at various conferences held around the country. After three years of its implementation, a senior lawyer's comment at a recent conference proved my worst fears—'The IB Code is one of the most ill-conceived pieces of legislation.'

This could have been prevented if a Transparent dialogue would have transpired between the industry and the government. Sadly, as usual, instead of the corporate world—which would be the most affected by the proposed legislation taking an active part in discussions at the drafting stage, it was the professional and services sector, having little knowledge of the practical issues plaguing Indian industry that got in the driver's seat, and the IB Code was born in December 2016 to address the long drawn process of revival/ closure of industries in distress, with little to no input from industry itself!

Despite all its good intentions, the IB Code, as the ICU for sick industries, has killed more companies than it could revive. Except in a few media-centric and well-known cases, it has failed to tackle the menace of NPAs (non-performing assets) in the banking system. The manner in which IB Code has been implemented, by blatantly discriminating against promoters, ignoring the interests of shareholders as well as the other day to day stakeholders, has had its negative impact on a very large number of operational and otherwise viable Indian companies leading to large scale job losses creating a very high level of rural distress, thus further impacting our economy, in addition to creating a new avenue of corruption.

We are still waiting for a mindset change in our bureaucracy whereby Indians are treated with dignity instead of as second class citizens in our own country.

We are waiting for Police Reforms.

We are waiting for Judicial Reforms.

We are waiting for Economic Reforms.

We are waiting for Educational Reforms.

We are waiting for Rule of Law.

We are waiting for the days when Public Policy is informed by Empirical and Evidence based data.

Without Transparent Dialogue and Constructive Criticism amongst ourselves, how will we achieve the India of our dreams and aspirations? When instead of our government bodies supporting us, keep trying to exploit us—can the 21st century really belong to India?

Such a regressive attitude has resulted in the fact that for the past seventy years, India has lost most of its meritorious students to the western world. Thanks to the continued Corruption, Nepotism, crude Educational standards and facilities, Political Dominance, Opaque systems and Legally-Mandated Harassment denying them their rightful place in India people like Abhijit Banerjee, Manu Prakash, Kalpana Chawla, Narinder Singh Kapany, Salman Rushdie, S. Chandrasekhar, Lakshmi Mittal, Indra Nooyi, Sundar Pichai, Satya Nadella (the list is endless!)—and so so many more instead of working and creating wealth, technology and progress for India within India; have left for countries that are more interested in their merits, potential, and inner drive than their surnames and bank balances. Consequently, while the developed world—led by the USA and the UK—enjoys the expertise, knowledge and progressive attitude from their adopted citizens of Indian origin to lead their Economies, India has lagged behind having lost its brightest minds to the western world.

A strong and positive government can create pathways to our progress, but only We the People of India can create a successful and happy India—full of talented, hard-working, critical thinking and wealth-creating Indians.

13

GUJARAT NRE—THE WEALTH CREATOR

The Gujarat NRE Group is one of the largest wealth creators of the country. It has been adjudged the fourth best performing stock on Indian bourses for a decade (2000-2010); it has had an unprecedented track record of rewarding its 2 lac+ public shareholders handsomely in addition to safeguarding the interest of all its stakeholders; it is the first and only Indian company to acquire and operate two premium hard coking coal mines in Australia successfully. Our ethical and prosperous venture has thus been instrumental in cementing the friendship ties between Australia and India, in addition to building a highly prestigious image for India and all Indians in Australia, while creating a niche for Aussie businesses and universities in India. Various awards given by the local communities—Australian and the expat Indian; the New South Wales government and the Australian government bear testimony to this fact.

Author with Hon. Morris Iemma, the then Premier of NSW and Indian community leaders.

Author with Brett Lee and Hon. Barry O'Farrell, the then Premier of NSW.

I hereby declare the appointment
in an honorary capacity
of

Arun Kumar Jagatramka

on behalf of New South Wales, Australia,
to promote the economic and cultural interests of the State as

Sydney Ambassador
to India

Premier of New South Wales
This 16th day of April in the year of 2008

The year 2004 was a watershed year for many of us in the steel industry. From the traditional price range of US\$ 50 to US\$ 90 until 2003 suddenly met coke prices broke all past records and predictions to cross US\$ 450! In tandem, coking coal also became scarce and its prices crossed US\$ 200 as against previous highs of around US\$ 60s. Against this backdrop of ongoing scarcity added to the astronomically higher prices of coking coal, it was akin to finding Kuber's wealth when I was offered the opportunity to own and operate a premium hard coking coal mine in Australia. After a careful due diligence of the historical mine with at least 2 decades more of coal left to be mined, I acquired the first coking coal mine in Australia in October 2004, with the second one soon thereafter.

Both mines were historically significant being the oldest operating coal mines in Australia, but this also meant that the old areas had been fully mined out with infrastructure and mining equipment long past their expiry date. And so for us, it was an exciting prospect to develop afresh and make new entry points and roadways to access new areas of coal reserves to begin and sustain mining for the next decade. This required patience, a host of approvals for the new development and massive capital expenditure in mine development as well as acquiring new and modern mining machineries. We were set for the long haul.

Initially, we relied on the strength of the Indian parent Gujarat NRE Coke Ltd. for funding with a mix of equity and debt amounting to more than 700 million AUD. However, we realised that the Indian Rupee Balance Sheet has severe limitations in financing overseas hard currency expenditure. And so we decided to list the Australian arm separately. Now the Australian subsidiary could raise finance on its own balance sheet though backed by the corporate guarantee from the Indian parent.

But, as the famous saying goes, man proposes, but god disposes. The Global Financial Crisis hit us in September 2008. The sudden mistrust in the global banking system led to total chaos in most businesses around the world. Consequently the Indian coke industry entered a downturn in October 2008, which got further prolonged due to the policy paralysis in the Indian government post the CWG scam in 2010–11, thereby affecting the ability of the Indian company to support its overseas operations. Adding fossil fuel to the financial fire, the Australian government in mid-2011 dealt a very serious blow to the Aussie coal mining industry with the sudden unplanned introduction of the carbon tax. Even though the proposed tax was futuristic and might not have had any actual cash impact on us, the psychological impact on investors led to drying up of all major sources of finance for the industry. Suddenly, the mining operations found itself cash starved right when we had geared up to ramp up production! Within a span of two years—between 2011 and 2013, our coal production had jumped three times from 60,000 tonnes a month in 2011 to more than two lac tonnes per month in 2013 with plans to produce close to five lac tonnes per month within next four years.

This massive increase in production required us to tie up with customers for the increased coal production. With the expected increase in infrastructure projects and thus consequent growth of the Indian steel industry, India was an obvious and natural market. We started exploring our options for tying up the future offtake with a strong steel production company with the ability to support part of the massive investment required for such an increase. However, the downturn in India affected most industries with the steel industry also in a bad shape and almost all Indian steel producers struggling for liquidity. So it was a huge surprise when early in 2011, apparently to meet its growing coking coal requirements, JSPL, an Indian steel producer started taking an interest in our mines and made several overtures to invest in them to secure offtake at reasonable prices!

An old Hindi saying goes,

जाकी रही भावना जैसी, प्रभु मूरत देखी तिन तैसी

(People will appear to you the way you perceive them to be.)

As such, JSPL became the natural choice for having a long-term relationship as an investor-cum-offtake partner. Consequently, in mid-2012, the initial share subscription-cum-offtake agreement was done, with the Indian steel producer introduced as a minority stakeholder in the Australian company. In personal meetings and discussions, the promoter of JSPL expressed his complete disinterest in taking over management control, while JSPL continued to acquire shares through the open market! The Gujarat NRE group was the majority stakeholder with 64% equity in the Australian company. Their unusually large stock acquisition on the open market resulted in the company's stock becoming almost illiquid, and the public holding reduced to 4% (!), so basically, the little funds that we had access to was also dried up by JSPL's actions, directly affecting our ability to raise emergency cash from other investors.

Again I approached the promoter of JSPL to understand his goals with regard to his future interest in the company and the mines. Again he was categorical in his disinterest in taking over. When I asked for further funding to ensure timely payment of weekly wages, he negotiated a majority stake, making it clear that he required and expected my continued participation. To protect the jobs of 500 plus employees, the Gujarat NRE Group allowed JSPL to get majority control of the company without seeking any payment for the immense amount of money, time, and energy that I have spent in building the Australian company. Now JSPL invested in fresh equity of the company at a much lower price compared to the valuation and the mines' potential, while its promoter was personally assuring us that the much needed financial support would be provided immediately! Multiple newspaper reports reveal the reality behind these promises.

Thus, the young company was forced to the brink of bankruptcy, and its potential investor instead of investing its funds in the promised support, acquired the entire company! I was fighting to keep the mines running, to ensure my employees were not made redundant, and to contribute to the beauty that is Wollongong. But with the situation so badly messed up, I finally took my exit, even though I firmly believed that the mines had a great future potential. The management is an important part of a business entity, but it is nothing without the employees, and so as always, following my policy of transparency with all my employees, I tendered my resignation letter explaining the entire situation in detail to all the employees. A copy of the said email is reproduced below:

Arun Kumar Jagatramka

From:	Arun Kumar Jagatramka
Sent:	14 February 2014 08:13
To:	SanjaySharma (sharma@gujaratnre.com.au)
Cc:	Jasbir Singh (jasbir.singh@jindalsteel.com); maurice.anghie@yahoo.com.au; afirek@orpheusenergy.com.au
Subject:	Resignation

To

The Company Secretary

Gujarat NRE Coking Coal Ltd

We all know that business means earning profits and creating wealth for its stakeholders. But despite this most important profit motive behind all our actions, I strongly believe that business is not just about making money. It is more about creating accessible and functional wealth that can be used to make better and happier lives for those directly involved as well as for the community that the business operates in.

This philosophy has been the cornerstone of my career, and for 17 years through the ups and downs of the volatile coal market, I have managed to uphold this belief. Both, in India and Australia I have strived and managed to bring balance and a steady economy to the communities that I have operated in.

The Gujarat NRE group has always invested in the happiness and the betterment of the lives of the people around. Thus, the group has sponsored primary schools and sports, built sanitation and electric facilities and temples, invested in windmills and Industrial Training Institutes (ITIs), and encouraged charities that help people with special needs, both in India and Australia. Personally, I have also done pioneering work to address the corruption in India, by creating awareness in the youth through seminars and contests and finding potential solutions.

As an Indian, I have built the confidence and respect for my country and country people in foreign shores and as an Indian Australian built a niche for Australian businesses in India and vice-versa by spreading the advantages of investing and working in Australia and with Australians.

Coal prices have always been volatile, with sharp changes in the graph but this should not translate into volatility in peoples' lives. I have continuously tried to cushion the jobs of those working for my company from drastic changes in the market.

In a downturn it is very easy to calculate the loss on a per ton basis of the coal produced and shipped. It is equally easy to shut down or cut jobs and lower production. But this is not conducive for a business with the intent and strength to stay and weather storms.

With emergency measures of redundancy during a downturn, in the longer term, the company in particular and the community in general loses out. If the company continues production in a downturn, it might be losing money in the short term, but ultimately with a continued permanent workforce, it would be able to recoup the loss much faster when the upturn returns and grow rapidly.

This has been my reason for continuing the operations of the company and to continue production despite the market being low and the prices going down while trying to cut costs on all fronts.

A few years ago, I had adopted the slogan 'Cut Costs to Save Jobs, do not Cut Jobs to Save Costs.'

And so, despite the downturn, despite not getting any funding on time, despite the humongous cash crunch, I always ensured timely payments for my employees besides not forcing a single person out of his job in last so many years.

Gujarat NRE Coking Coal Ltd. (GNCCL) was the Australian subsidiary of Gujarat NRE Coke Ltd. the largest Met Coke producing company of India. GNCCL owned and operated 2 premium hard coking coal mines in Australia. For 9 years GNCCL successfully developed and built these mines, which still has a potential of more than 20 years of mine life. In these 9 years GNCCL also received the unstinted support and love of the local community due to its transparent and honest approach.

In 2012, GNCCL envisaged the need for increased capital infusion to fund its mine development and expansion plans. Mine development is a capital intensive exercise. This required huge investment which could only be met by a mix of debt and equity, but it was necessary and imperative to help serve the long term purpose of preserving jobs and GNCCL's potential.

Mr Naveen Jindal had long been professing an interest in investing in the GNCCL mines to me. And thus as part of the capital raising exercise, the parent Gujarat NRE group introduced Mr Jindal's company JSPL as a minority stakeholder by offering them about 10% equity with an option to offtake coking coal from its mines in mid-2012.

Finding value in the company and its coal assets, JSPL continued acquiring shares through open market purchase. In January, 2013, Jindal group made an open offer for the Company, but even at that time during a personal meeting with me, Mr Jindal was categorical that he was interested only in buying shares from the market and was not looking to take over management control. In view of the Gujarat group holding around 64% equity the same was not possible as well. To prove himself, Jindal group allowed the open offer to be lapsed in March itself after they had acquired most of the shares held by outsiders and Mr Naveen Jindal continued to maintain that he was not interested in taking over management from me. Jindal group ended up acquiring 31.49% equity in the company with the result that the company's stock became almost illiquid on ASX with public holding reduced to less than 4%. This was a circumstance forced upon me and most unexpected.

The falling coal prices due to the drawn out global recession and a strong Australian dollar finally affected the daily cash flow of the company. The external global financial environment had been equally worse, preventing any further and timely funding from the banks. With poor liquidity in stock due to open offer by Jindal group, the company did not have many options to raise equity from the market.

I approached Mr Jindal to persuade him to make a capital investment and for his personal pledge of support. He was categorical that he did not want Jindal group to take over the management of the company but wanted to make a major investment in the company. He promised to infuse sufficient funds by way of additional equity in the company and loan facilities. He negotiated a majority stake and the right to appoint a director to the board and the CFO to control finances. He made it clear that he required and expected the continued participation of Gujarat group and for myself to continue to manage the company till the mines get into full production. He promised me an exit after selling our stake at a proper valuation.

With that pledge I was (and remain) confident as to the continued operations of the Company and the safeguarding of the jobs of 500 men employed in the company. To comply with various regulatory guidelines, there was no formal agreement between Jindal group and myself.

The share placement deal has been approved by the shareholders at a general meeting on 16th October 2013. Jindal received 328.5 million new shares at A$ 20 cents, as well as 328.5 million unlisted transferable options which shall be exercisable for nil consideration within a period of 5 years from the date of issue of the option. I believe that price to be lower than the market would expect if Jindal's intended support had been disclosed properly.

As a result of the introduction of the fresh equity into the company the holding of Jindal Group then increased to 44.68% and that of Gujarat Group reduced to 51.65%. Further on exercise of the options, Jindal's holding increased to 53.62% & Gujarat NRE's holding reduced to 43.30%.

It needs to be mentioned that, the Gujarat NRE group agreed to allow Jindal to get majority control of the company without seeking any payment and at a much lower price compared to the valuation and the mines' potential only for a consideration and commitment that the much needed financial support would be provided by the Jindal group immediately in July/August to ensure its solvency. The parent Gujarat NRE group has invested more than 700 million dollars in the form of equity and loans raised on its corporate guarantee. The expectation was that Jindal would match and exceed that commitment.

It was agreed that no further equity issue would be required until 31st March 2015 based on the expected financial support from Jindal and thereafter if any such issue is undertaken at any time then the same would not be at a price less than A$ 20 cents so as to ensure due protection of interest of all minority shareholders.

Of particular importance was the timing of further funding and out of $66 million, it was agreed that $45 million would be advanced by Jindal immediately after the date of signing the binding term sheet to take care of pressing creditors and put the GNCCL operations back on track asap.

However, as a major breach of trust, during the process of implementation of the proposed transaction Jindal group delayed the promised payments. GNCCL's board have agreed to modify the formal terms of agreement with Jindal despite my insistence that it be held to the bargain it made.

Understanding the sensitivity of timely payments of weekly wages, and my personal commitment towards such timely wage payment, Jindal purposefully forced the company in mid-September to run out of cash suddenly without notice, on more occasions than one, so that the management could not survive. That was the game plan on which they worked through September and October, forcing me to leave the company in their hands, without there ever been any deal with them in a commercial manner.

And even, when on 22nd October, 2013, my mother expired and I was in mourning for the customary 13-day period as per Hindu customs, I was personally harassed by Jindal, even during this personally difficult time.

This continued irresponsible behaviour has resulted in the GNCCL stocks plummeting from around 18 cents in June 2013 to scrounging between 6-7 cents in November 2013. This sharp devaluation in stock price was triggered by Jindal's refusal to confirm its support and appears to be part of the bigger plan to take advantage of GNCCL in successive rights issues at abnormally low valuation for the Company knowing fully well that given the negative publicity about the Company and the cash crunch, other shareholders cannot subscribe, allowing Jindal to increase its stake in the Company with highly prejudicial harm to all minority shareholders.

My intentions have always been genuine and that has been to save the company and to take care of the employees and the community. I did not seek any payment for ourselves in lieu of giving up the management forcibly, and had sacrificed everything for the sake of the company and the jobs of its employees.

Unfortunately, the Board of GNCCL has allowed Jindal to force the company into a situation where most employees were concerned about their future. Redundancies have been forced upon employees. Despite me continuing on the Board as a director and with my involvement in the Company as Executive Chairman for last so many years, I was not consulted about these redundancies at all which has been most painful for me personally during the entire saga.

It has not only been a story of great betrayal by Jindal against Gujarat NRE group and myself but also against Wollongong and the local community.

Recently, I have been accused of withholding my consent to the lodgement of the Prospectus, without valid basis, on the ground that this would have a potentially significant impact on the financial position and operations of the Company. I have also been threatened with various consequences if I continue to withhold my consent to lodgement of the Prospectus. In this respect, I wish to reiterate that I have requested accounting and legal opinion in support of the proposed capital raising for the benefit of the Board – I cannot see how that request is in any way unreasonable.

Considering the fact that the current stakeholders have put their faith in me, I believe it is my paramount duty to ensure GNCCL conduct itself appropriately by forcing Jindal to disclose its support in accordance with Mr Naveen Jindal's pledge to me (both in my personal capacity and as a Director of GNCCL). I would, once again, request the Board to take all necessary steps to ensure Jindal provides the expected support and that support is secured in a formal sense and disclosed to the market.

In the above background, I find that no purpose is being served by me continuing on the Board of GNCCL and as such by this email I hereby tender my resignation from the Board of Gujarat NRE Coking Coal Ltd and all its subsidiaries with immediate effect, and would request the Board for immediate acceptance and needful action.

Arun Kumar Jagatramka

On special request of JSPL's lawyers, I am appending below the response received:

Dear Arun,

Your decision to resign from Board of Gujarat NRE (and its subsidiaries) effective immediately on 14 February 2014 has been formally recorded by the remaining members of the Board on 17th Feburary, 2014.

Board has also reviewed various issues raised by you in the letter and specifically the following:

- ***My intentions have always been genuine and that has been to save the company and to take care of the employees and the community. I did not seek any payment for ourselves in lieu of giving up the management forcibly, and had sacrificed everything for the sake of the company and the jobs of its employees.***
- ***However, as a major breach of trust, during the process of implementation of the proposed transaction Jindal group delayed the promised payments. GNCCL's board have agreed to modify the formal terms of agreement with Jindal despite my insistence that it be held to the bargain it made.***

The new management did respond to my resignation, where all these facts were vaguely rejected, and rights were reserved by the new management of the Company to take appropriate legal action against me. The said action never came.

- *Understanding the sensitivity of timely payments of weekly wages, and my personal commitment towards such timely wage payment, Jindal purposefully forced the company in mid-September to run out of cash suddenly without notice, on more occasions than one, so that the management could not survive. That was the game plan on which they worked through September and October, forcing me to leave the company in their hands, without there ever been any deal with them in a commercial manner.*

- *Unfortunately, the Board of GNCCL has allowed Jindal to force the company into a situation where most employees were concerned about their future. Redundancies have been forced upon employees. Despite me continuing on the Board as a director and with my involvement in the Company as Executive Chairman for last so many years, I was not consulted about these redundancies at all which has been most painful for me personally during the entire saga*

Arun, I would like to inform that these assertions from your side are false, self serving and without basis and do not reflect your actions during the period when you were Executive Chairman of the Company.

Neither the Company nor the Jindal Group sees any benefit in responding to these matters raised in your letter other than to reject those assertions outright and to place you on notice that the decision not to engage in rejecting each assertion contained in your letter of resignation, or generally, should not be deemed to be any sort of agreement of or acquiescence to any of the matters raised in your letter.

The Company must also place you on notice that it reserves its rights and is considering its legal options to seek to recover from you any loss, cost or liability or damage incurred by the Company arising from your dissemination of your letter of resignation (and any future communication) to the Company employees.

Arun, in my respectful view, you have chosen to ignore your fiduciary duties owed by you to the Company and instead choose to obstruct, delay and compromise the success of the Company's proposed restructuring efforts in all possible manner like raising additional capital, restructuring of loans, redundancy effort and avoiding the Board meetings to the detriment of the Company and its members. As a matter of fact all your past and current actions are demonstrating that you have been favouring and acting to protect/benefit your Indian entity over this Company and other third party creditors.

In closing, your unilateral decision to resign from the Company and its related entities (the GNCCL Group) will not affect or be deemed to affect any rights the GNCCL Group has against you and for the avoidance of doubt, the GNCCL Group continues to reserve their respective rights against you and your related entities.

Jasbir Singh

You can imagine, there we were—our sleeves rolled up, ready to finally begin bearing the fruits of our hard labour, when the global banking system came crashing down taking everybody's liquidity with it. Then the respective governments in the countries that we call home decided to introduce policies without testing their efficacies on the already distressed economies, further demolishing any struggling chance we had. We stood at the coalface wondering which direction to take, when along comes this mysterious stranger—flush with funds in a time of global recession and offers his hand of friendship. What would you have done?

Although JSPL managed to acquire two operational hard coking coal mines, subsequent news reports did not depict the expected recovery and cash inflow/support—pay cuts and job losses, hazards found and the mines put under investigation for potential breaches of workplace safety laws, trend of increasing roof falls, catastrophic diesel engine failure, mining banned after worker hit, longwall blocked, opposed by residents, voluntary redundancy process, issued legal notice, debt restructure agreement, shareholder's ire, yet to obtain the necessary state and federal approvals, suspended from trade on the stock exchange, liabilities outweigh assets by more than AUD$ 748 million, company in dire financial position its own legal representative said, with revenue declining by 87 percent and a loss of AUD$ 762 million—these are just some of the sentences quoted verbatim from the newspapers. So in total, the management lost control, the employees lost their jobs, the public lost their money, and the community lost a thriving business.

According to newspaper reports, the NSW Resources Regulator initiated the first ever investigation into whether the Australian subsidiary controlled by an accused person under the Coal Scam is a fit and proper person to hold a coal mining license in NSW, Australia, while questions have been raised in the NSW, Australia Parliament about the feasibility of a person charge-sheeted on criminal corruption charges to be able to conduct business in Australia (You can watch the proceedings in the NSW Parliament in Australia on YouTube).

This is in stark contrast to my experiences and actions where I was awarded as the Illawarra Person of the Year in 2009 as well as nominated for the Australian of the Year award in 2010.

Courtesy: Illawarra Mercury

I mean, I did not even know the promoter of JSPL on a personal level. He himself came over extending a hand of financial help, and because I have always extended help to everyone with the only expectation of a happy relationship ahead, I did not expect such a weird turn of events.

Annoyingly, this is not the end of the sad saga.

In utter violation of ASIC regulations, Wollongong Coal Limited, (the Australian subsidiary), an ASX listed company, spent money to have my children including my daughters stalked by spies for the last few years, and this immoral act was declared in a judicial proceeding before the Supreme Court of New South Wales, Australia! (This only reconfirmed our apprehensions in this regard, by the way.)

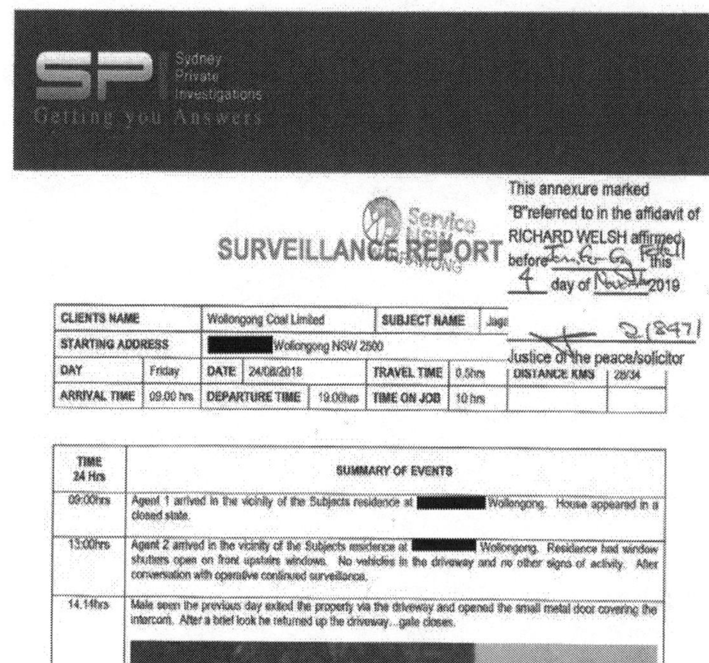

CLIENTS NAME		Wollongong Coal Limited		SUBJECT NAME	Jagi		
STARTING ADDRESS		Wollongong NSW 2500					
DAY	Friday	DATE	24/08/2018	TRAVEL TIME	0.5hrs	DISTANCE KMS	28/34
ARRIVAL TIME	09.00 hrs	DEPARTURE TIME	19.00hrs	TIME ON JOB	10 hrs		

TIME 24 Hrs	SUMMARY OF EVENTS
09:00hrs	Agent 1 arrived in the vicinity of the Subjects residence at ████ Wollongong. House appeared in a closed state.
13:00hrs	Agent 2 arrived in the vicinity of the Subjects residence at ████ Wollongong. Residence had window shutters open on front upstairs windows. No vehicles in the driveway and no other signs of activity. After conversation with operative continued surveillance.
14.14hrs	Male seen the previous day exited the property via the driveway and opened the small metal door covering the intercom. After a brief look he returned up the driveway...gate closes.

Multiple cases and FIRs were filed against almost all the senior managers of Gujarat NRE Coke in India including myself! All of them without any concrete basis!

In early 2018, an anonymous complaint was circulated to PMO, Income Tax Department, Ministry of Corporate Affairs (MCA), SEBI, the Serious Fraud Investigation Office (SFIO), CBI, ED, banks and many others. A copy of the same was sent to us by the MCA, and we replied in detail with annotations to each and every allegation (some of which were frankly unrealistic), effectively proving that the complaint was totally false and manufactured out of bad intentions against Gujarat NRE Coke Ltd. and myself.

Oddly, soon thereafter in mid–2018, another complaint (almost a copy-paste of the anonymous complaint sent earlier) was filed by one Krishna Kant Agarwal, a copy of which was sent to us by the SEBI seeking clarifications. Again we responded in detail proving each and every allegation in the complaint as false and without any basis. I also filed a defamation suit in the Calcutta High Court and got an injunction against Krishna Kant Agarwal from circulating such bogus complaints.

In India, there is no provision for government officers to provide reasons for initiating any enquiry and/or investigation on a citizen of India. The opacity of the investigation process makes it ripe for malafide and malicious misuse, leading to the present trust deficit in our system.

When our government officers can provide empirical evidence for the need to investigate a genuine suspect of wrongdoing—our government agencies will create trust for citizens in our government system. This will also have the added advantage of minimizing the malafide and corrupt investigations that misuse our government and our tax rupees.

Similarly, there is no provision for the timely closure of the files, leading to further delays and thus frustrations.

A truly successful business creates wealth and prosperity for everyone—from the promoter–entrepreneur who holds the maximum risk, to the employees who get to learn new skills while developing confidence in their original ones, to the communities that it operates in, generating resources, choices and thus development.

A business cannot thrive without the positive and active interest and participation of the communities that it operates in. When inept and heavy-handed business promoters try to simply extract and exploit without contributing anything back, it obviously results in not only bad business filled with undue stress, it also leads to corruption and thus crime.

The reason for Gujarat NRE Group's survival even under liquidation is simple. Trust and Transparency.

This has been further reinforced when even I was surprised to find a full length photograph and a positive reference to the work done by me for the local community in the special Australia Day cover story published recently by Illawarra Mercury on 25th January, 2020 more than 6 years after my exit.

OUR AUSSIE HEROES

BLOODIED BUT NEVER BOWED

weekender.

BULLET DODGED: Hawks shareholders Wayne Morris, Kyle Page and Richard Clifford celebrate the club's first Houdini act. **Picture: Sylvia Liber.**

BRIEF: Telco millionaire James Spenceley, pictured with with Hawks Chairman Peter Batimann in 2014, had a short stint as owner of the Illawarra club. **Picture: Andy Zakeli**

SAVIOUR: Arun Jagatramka Chairman with Wollongong Hawks Mat Campbell, after the Chair of Gujarat agreed to be the $1 million dollar Guarantor of the Hawks in the New NBL. **Picture: Dave Tease**

Courtesy: Illawarra Mercury

14

GUJARAT NRE—ALSO WAITING FOR ACHHE DIN

By October 2013, the industry was in such a bad shape, that Gujarat NRE was referred by bankers for CDR (corporate debt restructuring). CDR was supposed to be the mechanism for revival of companies in distress, but instead of achieving the desired objective, all it could achieve was its blatant misuse by the bankers as a tool to defer the provisioning for NPAs in their books with the result that very few companies could successfully come out of CDR. And in most cases the problem was simply postponed while allowing the bankers to carry their loan exposure as a standard asset in their books even though the company remained largely non-functional(!) while the loan outstandings kept on mounting with compounded interest without generating any profit.

In our case, the met coke industry in addition to being in severe downturn due to the sorry state of the steel industry was also suffering due to the dumping of met coke from China.

Our efforts in getting the Government of India to impose anti-dumping duty on the import of Chinese coke in a timely manner fell on deaf ears and it took almost two years from our making an application in October 2014 to November 2016 when the anti-dumping duty was finally imposed. By that time, for Gujarat NRE, CDR had failed. The cognitive distortion of 'all-or-nothing' thinking of the bankers had resulted in its accounts finally classified as NPA by the bankers and with continued sluggishness in the industrial scenario, it seemed like it was the end of the road for Gujarat NRE. To add salt to our wounds, the Central government suddenly announced demonetization of high value currency notes in November 2016 just days before the imposition of anti-dumping duty! The resultant paralysis in trade and industry for the next few months snatched away whatever little benefit we could have reaped from the imposition of the anti-dumping duty.

Having failed in our efforts to sell the family silver in the company, namely, the wind mills in 2015 and unable to convince the banks in accepting the revival plan submitted by me in early 2016, it was in the last week of March 2017 that I decided to test the efficacy of the newly introduced IB Code and proposed to the Board of Gujarat NRE Coke to decide on referring the company for corporate insolvency resolution process (CIRP) under the IB Code. In doing so, various factors weighed on me including imposition of anti-dumping duty on met coke from China since November 2016, the stated objectives and preamble to the IB Code, and the potential revival of the industry post the downturn created by demonetization in November 2016. All these factors led to my full confidence in being able to revive the company if the additional unsustainable debt burden due to interest on interest compounded monthly for the last few years while the company was non-operative could be taken care of in a timely manner.

In the last week of March 2017, I approached the Kolkata Bench of National Company Law Tribunal (NCLT) for getting Gujarat NRE admitted to the IB Code under Section 10 thereof. We were one of the first big cases under the new law and perhaps the only one of our size till date who decided to do so suo moto instead of being dragged by lenders like in most other cases.

The NCLT, Kolkata Bench, passed its order on 7 April 2017 admitting our petition and putting Gujarat NRE into CIRP. Taking the preamble to the IB Code at its face value, we had steered ourselves in what was largely uncharted territory those days and were quite hopeful of successful resolution and revival of GNCL given its clean track record and its fundamental viability not being in doubt. However, the bankers who were entrusted with the maximum responsibility under the IB Code to safeguard their own interests as well as the interests of all other stakeholders, continued with their destructive and restrictive ALL-OR-NOTHING thinking and acted in the most irresponsible manner by participating in the COC meetings only to play around and waste precious time instead of focusing on the revival of GNCL and safeguarding—their own interests, interest of other creditors, and the 2 lac public shareholders—whose fate was handed over in their hands by the architects of the IB Code. They seemed unable to comprehend the strict time limit of 180 days for the entire process. The IB Code held them accountable for saying 'Yes' to a resolution plan, but it refused to hold them accountable for an inexplicable 'No'. Besides, the Code did not provide the bankers with any sort of immunity for their actions even if taken in good faith to revive the Company as mandated by the

IB Code. Thus leading to their casual attitude and indecisive behaviour which resulted in the compulsory liquidation of GNCL under the IB Code on expiry of 270 days, putting 1,178 employees at the risk of losing their employment and jeopardising the livelihood of more than 10,000 families indirectly dependent on our operations at that time, besides total loss of investment owned by more than 2 lac public shareholders.

Considering the large employee strength of the company, the NCLT couldn't pass the usual liquidation order of discharging all employees. Rather in a Legal first, the NCLT, Kolkata Bench, passed a landmark order on 11 January 2018 putting GNCL into liquidation as a going concern and asked the liquidator to try and sell the company as a going concern to safeguard the employment of so many people. It was a historic judgement in a sense that there was no provision in the applicable laws for such an order at the relevant time. However, the regulatory authorities took note of the same and within a few months amended the regulations to make the order passed on 11 January legally compliant.

Having been successful in saving the livelihood of all my employees who are as much responsible in the success of Gujarat NRE as I am, I began to explore various options to somehow revive the company and bring it out of the unjust liquidation. My background as a chartered accountant with a keen interest in the company law came to my rescue once again. I realized that Section 230 of the Companies Act, 2013 could be used to propose a Scheme of Compromise and with the support of all the creditors of the company, Gujarat NRE could be taken out of liquidation with a super majority. It was no doubt a herculean task, given that as against the process of CIRP where we needed only one class of creditors being members of the COC to be convinced and vote on the proposal, Section 230 was much more stringent with the requirement of getting consent by a super majority for each class of stakeholders separately. However, having faith in our hard work, the goodwill that we have earned for the past two decades and my track record of ethically managing the company and treating all stakeholders in a fair and transparent manner, I set out on the path with my full focus on taking the company out of liquidation.

A promoter nurses a company with his sweat and blood, like a mother takes care of her infant, and ensures that the company survives and grows despite all odds. It is unimaginable that he could ever be accused of running down the very company that was built by him. Yes, in a few cases the black sheep in the industry do engage in fraudulent conduct and amass vast personal fortune or indulge in criminal diversion at the cost of their own company and waste public funds, and they need to be tackled strongly. But the irony is that using their ill-gotten wealth, the corrupt have been successful in evading the system in various ways while those of us who have been subject to external factors resulting in NPAs and refused to adopt illegal practices have been harassed and hounded because we refuse to pay extortionary bribes!

The manner in which the IB Code has been implemented where the promoter is treated as an outcast having no voice in the revival of his company that he has built, has done the most serious harm to our financial and industrial ecosystem where genuine potentially viable companies have been consigned to the gallows for no fault of their promoters, and their genuine efforts to revive the company have been simply ignored!

In February 2018, when I had proposed the compromise scheme under Section 230 of the Companies Act, 2013, the section was unheard of and I had to convince even my own legal team that we could do this within the boundaries of law. But now, another goalpost was added! Suddenly the whole country decided to stereotype all promoters as chor(!), negating all legal provisions provided to us by the Constitution of India of not discriminating against any criteria—the absolutely discriminating Section 29A was introduced into the IB Code. It made the promoter an alien in his own house! Now everybody who I talked to wanted me—and actually advised me—not to do anything in my own name and nominate any person who could be trusted to propose the scheme for revival of the company as a third party! *This proves so effectively that discrimination begets corruption!*

Even senior counsels of the Calcutta High Court who we approached to move my petition before the NCLT to propose the scheme under Section 230 were of the view that the scheme should be proposed by a third party and as a promoter I should not try to do so. It was common knowledge that in almost all cases, promoters were putting up Benaami persons to propose the Resolution Plan in the IB Code, and I was also supposed to do the same!

It is not by accepting the wrong that a human is granted happiness and success, neither by destroying and blowing up systems that create the wrongs—the road to happiness and success is filled with critical thinking humans trying to find solutions to our problems. I refused to give in to the wrong and dishonourable suggestion to use Benaami and went ahead and filed the petition under my own name, and even somehow managed to convince a legal counsel in Kolkata to represent me before the NCLT and propose the scheme for the revival of Gujarat NRE.

NCLT, Kolkata, successfully passed its orders around 15 May 2018 allowing us to convene separate meetings of all stakeholders of Gujarat NRE Coke Ltd. to consider and vote for the proposed scheme under Section 230 of the Companies Act, 2013.

I had broken the first barrier in the chakravyuh.

The notices for four separate meetings of different stakeholders were despatched in the second week of June 2018, and it was decided to convene the meetings on 16 July 2018. I travelled extensively in this period both within as well as outside the country to meet various creditors as well as shareholders in order to explain the scheme and get them on board. The bankers, of course, could see strong merit in the scheme where their recovery could be at least four times the uncertain amount to be realized as the ultimate liquidation value, which could be more in the form of equity upside since the secured bankers also hold around 34 per cent equity in Gujarat NRE. But they were almost categorical in their response that they would like me to put up a Benaami person to front me, as their system would not support the promoter in any event! I told them that any use of Benaami was out of question as far as I was concerned and if they had any other investor for the company, I would fully support the person for the sake of my employees and my shareholders, but otherwise they would have to support me since as long as I could I would keep fighting for our revival and would not allow the company that I have built over my lifetime to go down the drain for their own prejudices. Winners never quit and quitters never win.

Unsecured creditors were happy but as usual *Yeh Dil Maange More* (The heart wants more). Most of them could appreciate the great value in the potential upside with existing shareholders but still wanted a much bigger piece of the cake. I had to explain to them that of the existing shareholders 34 per cent was secured lenders having first charge on the company while around 42 per cent was held by more than two lac public shareholders whose interest was also paramount for me and as such they needed to look at their own recovery howsoever small as against NIL recovery in liquidation. However, I did commit to explore ways to increase their recovery, which I ultimately did in the revised scheme later on.

I also held several meetings with public shareholders in various cities across the country to explain this herculean task that I had put myself up for and gauge their mood and get their support in reviving Gujarat NRE. These meetings were real eye-openers. For a man who had been listening to a constant demand for benaami person in lieu of himself, to find my shareholders' trust, support and confidence still with me reaffirmed the old dictum that Lakshmiji might be fickle, but vishwas—goodwill earned with continued honest work and transparent dialogue is forever. I was completely floored to find the level of confidence, respect and support that I had from all of Gujarat NRE's/my shareholders across all the cities that I held such meetings. They reiterated their whole-hearted support for me personally and despite losing heavily due to the company having gone into liquidation were highly appreciative of all that I had done for rewarding the shareholders when the company was making profits and the transparency shown by me through regular communications and physical interactions, which was unheard of by any other promoter in the country.

After completing all these meetings by early July 2018, we were eagerly waiting for Dday, that is, 16 July 2018, for the 4 meetings convened to decide on our future, but then out of the blue around 12th July a day before the e-voting was to open, we were served with an ex parte stay order on all the meetings granted by the NCLAT, New Delhi, based on an application filed by Jindal Steel & Power Ltd which was having an unsecured claim over the company constituting around 0.5 per cent of the total claims and otherwise ineligible to make any kind of objections to the said scheme in terms of the applicable law. The notice for the meetings had been served well in advance—in mid-June— that is, almost a month had passed for anybody with a genuine grievance to approach the courts and seek appropriate relief. Even otherwise, in recent years with technology in our hands, the courts insist on service of notice at the least on email and are generally reluctant to grant any sort of ex parte stay (that is, without listening to the other party). But in this case disconcerting questions regarding our judicial system have been thrown up due to the manner in which the NCLAT judges have put a stay to the meetings that had been convened with due process of law.

Of course such destructive acts took their toll on the entire ecosystem— with the potential revival of our company, and the recovery of banking dues taking a back seat, while we sat and watched with horror the present faces of our judiciary.

It is frustrating that our democracy till now has no safeguards against malicious prosecutions and no punishments against the abuse of legal process to deter such corrupt and unnecessary cases which further inhibit and delay justice in our already clogged up judicial system.

Meanwhile, we continued our efforts to convince the NCLAT to allow me to reconvene the meetings under Section 230 and refocus on the revival of the company. However, with the entire nation's load on one single bench of the NCLAT, the matter dragged on for more than a year. During this period, however, the IB Code kept on undergoing various changes due to— the amendments in the code by the government, the issue of new/amended guidelines and regulations by the Insolvency and Bankruptcy Board of India (IBBI), the judicial pronouncements both by the NCLAT and the Supreme Court of India, and, above all, a general mindset change where the dirty effects of liquidation were well understood by both the regulators as well as the courts. Generally by the end of January 2019, both Supreme Court and the NCLAT were fully convinced that India could not afford liquidation of viable companies and started advocating the use of Section 230 of the Companies Act, 2013 before actually initiating the liquidation process.

What an irony! Gujarat NRE Coke Ltd., despite being the pioneer in the matter having invoked Section 230 before anybody else could even think about it, is still stuck for want of a clear direction on the pending appeal before the NCLAT. While the same NCLAT is asking all liquidators in every order of liquidation passed by it since February 2019 to explore options for revival of the company under Section 230 of the Companies Act, 2013 before proceeding with the liquidation, and at the same time making it amply clear that as section 230 is under the Companies Act, the promoters are fully eligible and could not be debarred under the discriminating section 29A of the IB Code from proposing a scheme under Section 230 of the Companies Act as the two acts were separate!

It is pertinent to note that the company despite being in liquidation since January, 2018 still remains a going concern and still has almost 1,000 employees on its rolls who are getting paid their monthly dues as well as all other emoluments regularly out of the operational cash flow of the company, and its plants remain operational. Such a large number of employees in its continued employment proves the faith of all the employees in the management and their confidence in the future viability of the business of

Gujarat NRE Coke Ltd. Had there been any incidents of fraud, etc., in the company, most of the employees would have left long back, and in any event the company would have struggled to find adequate cash flow to pay all the employees and keep the plant operational even during liquidation for such a long time. The company also boasts of having one of the lowest attrition rates in the country with the majority of its employees having been employed for more than ten years with the company.

Since 2013, Gujarat NRE Coke has been subjected to multiple forensic audits, regular monthly concurrent audits, regular stocks and receivables audits by independent auditors appointed by banks and the liquidator. The liquidator also got a forensic audit done specially to investigate all the allegations made in the anonymous complaint letters. None of these audit reports have ever pointed out any major discrepancy or fraud in Gujarat NRE.

The line between a regular business caught in the fluctuating Global and Domestic economic cycles, and a fraud and/or a willful defaulter needs to be redrawn. We do need to differentiate between frauds and failures. Every business failure cannot and should not be labelled as fraud. To punish the promoter for business failure which are at times beyond his control for various external factors is against the principle of natural justice. It would kill the entrepreneurship in the country as people would shy away from setting an industry. Instead of developing India, we would be going back in time when only foreign businesses and big corporates owned the country's resources, while the common Indian citizen remained workers and employees with no say.

Gujarat NRE Coke LTD. has been under liquidation since 11th January, 2018. During the 2 years' period of liquidation until 31st December, 2019, it has perhaps created history by remaining operational and having achieved a turnover of more than Rs. 1,000 CRORES!

This is categorical, and undeniable, proof of not only the viability and the real potential of Gujarat NRE, but also the trustworthy, integrity and corruption-free structure of the company that I have given my life to.

We retain the full faith and support of our 1000-strong workforce who have continued their employment in the company. Through my periodical updates and transparent dialogue with them, I feel blessed to find out that Gujarat NRE retains the faith and support of our shareholders—two lac strong. The support from all—our employees, our suppliers and dealers, and our shareholders—has given me the strength to persevere and make Gujarat NRE a wealth creator of the twenty-first century too.

EPILOGUE

Systemic and Petty Corruption, or as I like to call them—Extortionary Corruption still holds on to us, tight in its vice-like grip. More than collusive corruption, it is Extortionary Corruption that torments the Common Indian Citizen. The ₹500 that we give to the traffic policeman to look the other way, the under-the-table bribe given to the municipal officer to clean the drains from our street, the stay-away bribe given to local authorities to stay away from our newly opened shop, the 'chai-paani' given to the taxman for leaving our office so that we can go home at the end of the day after a surprise 'raid' are a few examples of extortionary corruption. The day-to-day amenities and needs mandated by the Constitution of India still feel like a climb to the Mount Everest—doable, but energy-draining. Our government institutions are still unapproachable and provide for frustrating experiences due to their discretionary and monopolistic powers that they hold since colonial times. Disturbingly extortionary corruption prices have seen a rise despite the crackdown on Collusive Corruption by the present government. The increased pressure and high risk of being caught and prosecuted has made these corrupt officers demand larger amounts than before.

This book is the next step in my campaign for a corruption-free India. It is an attempt to exhibit how one can make Integrity a bedfellow in a world dominated by corruption. It is the balance sheet of an honest Indian businessman.

I hope you will join me in creating a happy and successful India.

Appendix 1

NEWSPAPER ARTICLES

THE ECONOMIC TIMES | MONDAY | 17TH AUGUST 2009

'Chalta hain culture & herd mentality suppress talent, promotes mediocrity'

Arun Kumar Jagatramka

WHAT does the oft-repeated term CSR mean? What makes a corporate citizen stand out as a socially conscious one? What are the responsibilities that a good corporate should bear to be one that can be recognised as a socially responsible corporate citizen? Is the entire premise about paying lip service by adding platitudes that mean nothing and filling in a few paragraphs in the website or the brochure? Surely, for a corporate, whose raison d'etre is to add value and create wealth, esoteric concepts like these should not divert the attention from its basic functions. Then why is the din so deafening?

Is CSR all about photo opportunities then? Politically correct picture post cards posted from the slums of the city? Pictures of smiling malnutrition, of pot-bellied children who do not have access to two square meals a day, savouring candies provided by a corporate as part of its annual function? Of the boss' wife unveiling the 'safe sanitation week' in collaboration with the officer's wife's institute that profess the virtues of sanitation to those who do not have access to it? It is not in my nature to belittle efforts of others, however trivial they may seem against the yardsticks of practicality. Far from it. I salute the efforts and honour the spirit behind each one of them.

It is just that I define the entire premise in different terms. My take is far more fundamental. The measures that I take and hope to continue taking are far more basic. And I try to approach the whole thing by virtue of being an Indian first. An Indian industrialist, if you may. I add the term industrialist because, as one, I have access not only to the requisite funds, but also to the management skill sets to ensure their optimal deployment and effective usage.

And, like a true corporate soldier, before going into the blitzkrieg, I assess the objective that has to be secured, the resources required to achieve the end, the means that have to be deployed and try to identify pitfalls on the way to achievement.

So what is the objective? To help create an India that our forefathers dreamt of. An India that has secured her rightful place in the League of Nations. More importantly, an India that has learnt how to hold her head high.

And what is the biggest obstacle on the path? An age-old value system, that has steadily corroded over the last couple of decades. We have a judiciary that is loaded by the legislature about the severity of punishment as opposed to certainty of punishment. We have a political system that is concerned merely about its own continuity by dividing the nation in terms of caste, creed, region, religion, colour and language so that it can play one group against the other for political gains. We have a bureaucracy where entry ensures continuity to eternity without accountability. All three of which have combined to create a nation which is run on the motto "chalta hai"! The reign of mediocrity that doesn't not allow talent to foster, for it is more profitable to be a part of the herd — be that the Muslim herd, or the Maharashtrian herd, or the Dalit herd, or the villager herd — than stand out as an Indian.

Naturally, this India is the hotbed of corruption. Whether a birth certificate or a death certificate, everything comes at a cost. The local police station, the municipal corporation, the registrar of companies, the Income Tax department, the department dealing with motor vehicles — are all fountainheads from where sprouts the hydra-headed monster called corruption. We jump up and down in joy when the lone politician is 'exposed' in a sting operation, but do nothing about tackling the malaise.

We clap our hands and move on. We move on because we do not think twice before jumping the traffic signal when there are no policemen around. We move on because we do not think twice before 'greasing' the odd palm, to move just that bit up in life. We move on, because we do not consider corruption an ill. We move on because, in this age of instant gratification, we too want things 'done'. We too want to get on with life and are willing to pay that 'extra' bit to achieve our ends. And here, I am talking of you and me.

The same you and me, who swore eternal revenge when the Mumbai terror attacks happened. The same you and me, us, who professed the idea of hot pursuit. 'Us', who heaped indignities on the politicians for having 'compromised' the security of the Nation. For having 'sold' national needs for pecuniary benefit. For having 'compromised' national security — the same you and me, who had looked the other way when a police constable's son had, over decades, grown into a 'don'. The same you and me who had not raised our voice when an unknown 'Indian' had let in 'his' consignment of deadly RDX for a 'fee'. The same you and me who use 'hawala' to evade a few rupees in taxes as we send money to our children studying abroad. The same hawala, that the mongers of terror use to finance attacks on the nation.

And it is here that I want to strike. Into the very heart of this apathetic, 'sanitised' thought process. It is not an easy task. Of injecting 'integrity' into the very consciousness of India, of every Indian. It is not an easy task. It is not impossible either. And I have taken it on me to spread the word.

The target is the future. Young impressionable minds that are awaiting ignition. It is my mission to ignite a million minds and ensure that they take the message forward, so that my children and their children can live in the India that our forefathers had dreamt of.

Jai Hind!

The author is also member-representative of Gujarat NRE-AMA Center for National Integrity, Ahmedabad

The Economic Times—17 August 2009

CHALTA HAIN CULTURE & HERD MENTALITY
SUPPRESS TALENT, PROMOTES MEDIOCRITY

What does the oft-repeated term CSR mean? What makes a corporate citizen stand out as a socially conscious one? What are the responsibilities that a good corporate should bear to be one that can be recognised as a socially responsible corporate citizen? Is the entire premise about paying lip service by adding platitudes that mean nothing and filling in a few paragraphs in the website or the brochure? Surely, for a corporate, whose raison d'etre is to add value and create wealth, esoteric concepts like these should not divert the attention from its basic functions. Then why is the din so deafening?

Is CSR all about photo opportunities then? Politically correct picture post cards posted from the slums of the city? Pictures of smiling malnutrition, of potbellied children who do not have access to two square means a day, savouring candies provided by a corporate as part of its annual function? Of the boss' wife unveiling the 'safe sanitation week' in collaboration with the officer's wife's institute that profess the virtues of sanitation to those who do not have access to it? It is not in my nature to belittle efforts of others, however trivial they may seem against the yardsticks of practicality. Far from it. I salute the efforts and I honour the spirit behind each one of them.

It is just that I define the entire premise in different terms. My take is far more fundamental. The measures that I take and hope to continue taking are far more basic. And I try to approach the whole thing by virtue of being an Indian first. An Indian industrialist, if you may, I add the term industrialist because, as one, I have access not only to the requisite funds, but also to the management skill sets to ensure their optimal deployment and effective usage.

And like a true corporate soldier, before going into the blitzkrieg, I assess the objective that has to be secured, the resources required to achieve the end, the means that have to be deployed and try to identify pitfalls on the way to achievement.

So what is the objective? To help create an India that our forefathers dreamt of. An India that has secured her rightful place in the League of Nations. More importantly, an India that has learnt how to hold her head high.

And what is the biggest obstacle on the path? An age-old value system, that has steadily corroded over the last couple of decades. We have a judiciary that is loaded by the legislature about the severity of punishment as opposed to certainty of punishment. We have a political system that is concerned merely about its own continuity by dividing the nation in terms of caste, creed, region, religion, colour and language so that it can play one group against the other for political gains. We have a bureaucracy where entry ensures continuity to eternity without accountability. All three of which have combined to create a nation which is run on the motto "chalta hai"! The reign of mediocrity that does not allow talent to foster, for it is more profitable to be a part of the herd—be that the Muslim herd, or the Maharashtrian herd, or the Dalit herd, or the villager herd—than standout as an Indian.

Naturally, this India is the hotbed of corruption. Whether a birth certificate or a death certificate, everything comes at a cost. The local police station, the municipal corporation, the registrar of companies, the Income Tax department, the department dealing with motor vehicles—are all fountain heads from where sprouts the hydra headed monster called corruption. We jump up and down in joy when the lone politician is 'exposed' in a sting operation, but do nothing about tackling the malaise.

We clap our hands and move on. We move on because we do not think twice before jumping the traffic signal when there are no policemen around. We move on because we do not think twice before 'greasing' the odd palm, to move just that bit up in life. We move on, because we do not consider corruption an ill. We move on, because, in this age of instant gratification, we too want things 'done'. We too want to get on with life and are willing to pay that 'extra' bit to achieve our ends. And here, I am talking of you and me.

The same you and me, who swore eternal revenge when the Mumbai terror attacks happened. The same you and me, us, who professed the idea of hot pursuit. 'Us', who heaped indignities on the politicians for having "compromised" the security of the Nation. For having 'sold' national needs for pecuniary benefit. For having 'compromised' national security—the same you and me, who had looked the other way when a police constable's son had, over decades, grown into a 'don'. The same you and me who had not raised our voice when an unknown 'Indian' had let in 'his' consignment of deadly RDX for a 'fee'. The same you and me who use 'hawala' to evade a few rupees in taxes as we send money to our children studying abroad. The same hawala, that the mongers of terror use to finance attacks on the nation.

And it is here that I want to strike into the very heart of this apathetic, 'sanitised' thought process. It is not an easy task. Of injecting 'integrity' into the very consciousness of India, of every Indian. It is not an easy task. It is not impossible either. And I have taken it on me to spread the word.

The target is the future. Young impressionable minds that are awaiting ignition. It is my mission to ignite a million minds and ensure that they take the message forward, so that my children and their children can live in the India that our forefathers had dreamt of.

Jai Hind!

Ethical Deficit to Trust Deficit...
Cushioning the Social Diseconomies....

For long we have been patting our own backs on stories of India rising and our ambition to clock double digit growth. It is true that we can still expect 9% growth in the long run, which probably might be one of the highest in the world. But a slight introspection would reveal that at present the momentum seems to be loosing its steam. The various corruption issues opening up like a can of worms is not only severely denting investor confidence, it has all the ammo to derail the much touted Indian growth story. The signs are ominous. FDI in India declined in this year. GDP growth is declining steadily to 7.7% in the second quarter of 2011. Investors are holding up investments, capital is locked up in projects, and negative signs post August / September 2010 is all encompassing. There is something in the air which is preventing any further movement, awaiting a big push for the return of the feel good factor. The mood is sombre, and the corporate earning figures have also not lifted up the spirit. Deep rooted corruption and total apathy of the common man in the system prevents an inclusive growth and is creating a bigger divide between the haves and the have nots which might result into India facing a Malthusian nightmare instead of reaping its demographic dividend.

The Government needs to get its act together and take some bold decisions to unshackle the system and induce further growth. The government should make some bold announcements to convey its willingness to come clean on matters of corruption and black money. We need an out of the box approach to achieve this. The tax rates should be lowered significantly. Specific moves like zero capital gains tax and 1% stamp duty on all real estate deals to encourage full value transactions is the need of the hour. Last time when we rationalized the tax system in 1985-86, all fears of loss of government revenue were put to rest when the actual tax collection was much higher by the lowering of taxes. We need a radical move from the government which dismantles the current rate provision.

Trust is a valuable social asset that forms the basis of democracy. Trust demands respect for the inherent value and rights of a human being. It is time for us to accept that while "taxes are the price we pay for civilization"- civilization cannot sustain itself without trust. Distrust kills transparency, creates divide and fuels maneuvering to suit ones motive. If a government distrusts its people, people are likely to reciprocate by distrusting the system. Reciprocity and cooperation increase in a trust based regime where people trust that others will indeed reciprocate.

Sadly in India it is this trust that is missing. Recent events have only pointed out the extent of this trust deficit and the lack of faith that people have in the laid down processes and the norms of democracy that we so proudly hold to with high esteem. The best way to promote trust is to promote procedural justice, legitimacy and identification which would create a sense of respect for the authorities among the mass and a belief that he is being trusted by the men in power.

The government should encourage voluntary compliance. Forced compliance is leading to a situation where there is no fear of getting caught but, leading to an easier route of not complying and when the turn comes of being scrutinized, one easily gets away with payouts - invariably payouts are a cheaper option than compliance in monetary terms, wherein both parties benefit. The prevailing raid raj and high handedness of agencies aided by the discretionary power inbuilt in our laws is one of the key reasons for lack of compliance. Voluntary disclosure should be encouraged; instill trust in the system which would ultimately result in much greater compliance. It is not a novel idea, our previous experiences illustrate that a lower tax system accompanied by self compliance will result into greater revenue collection, given our current improved e-governance. The developed countries in the world do not have the kind of forced compliance that we have in India, but they have much better compliance. Hence it is high time we change the existing system which is corrupt and not working in our favour and announce some forward looking measures in this regard. Trust based compliance with strict enforcement in case of any breach of this trust is the need of the hour.

The Government should empower and encourage public participation in the cleansing process. Economic offenders should be made public and the highest tax payers should be honoured. Repeat offenders should pay steep and certain penalties and repeat performers should be awarded. Our system provides overriding power to the enforcement agencies which leads to extortionary corruption. Policy correction can curb extortionary corruption. Moreover, it is extortionary corruption which affects the common man, the honest man. The tax laws should provide at least the minimum dignity to the tax payers.

Trust based compliance with strict enforcement in case of any breach of this trust is the need of the hour. This would make the tax system more robust, transparent and vibrant. The call is for freedom from being harassed by the authorities due to the huge discretionary power that they enjoy. We may look at diluting this excessive discretionary power to enable more trust and faith in the system.

As a one time exercise, we may also look at an amnesty scheme to clear off all backlogs and post that treat whosoever evades tax with strict enforcement. The proposed amnesty scheme may be treated differently from all the previous amnesty schemes, since we did not have the kind of technology and e-governance previously that we have today. Today with the prevalent 360o profiling, we can literally track all transactions and expenditures of any individual, particularly of the high net worth individuals. The amnesty scheme would only help a large section of willing citizens to come clean and honest, who have been living in the middle of corruption and deceit forced upon by the antediluvian tax system. Trust your citizen, and if he betrays your trust, punishment should be certain and exemplary.

Personally, I am against any amnesty scheme as it penalizes the honest. A three year limitation for any investigation or enforcement, which itself would clear more than 80% of the back log in the system and divert all our resources to more recent ones to get results instead of motivated grave digging of evergreen cases without any convictions may be a better option. This would also free our citizens from a lifelong fear of the unknown, of being persecuted for things they may never have done or known and don't have enough time or money to fight the system in which they have been caught.

Today we need a bold message through action from the government that it intends to fight corruption and bring in transparency in governance. The government needs to walk the extra mile to announce some big ticket reforms to bring in some cheer in the investment climate. The present status quo needs to go and the country needs to start moving.

— Arun Kumar Jagatramka

The Economic Times—14 November 2011

ETHICAL DEFICIT TO TRUST DEFICIT ...
CUSHIONING THE SOCIAL DISECONOMIES ...

We must learn to trust….. For several centuries, Indians have been brainwashed to distrust other Indians. This saps national energy. Distrust kills initiative. Distrust compels people to manoeuvre and manipulate. Trust and transparency stimulates entrepreneurship.

For long we have been patting our own backs on stories of India rising and our ambition to clock double digit growth. It is true that we can still expect 9 per cent growth in the long run, which probably might be one of the highest in the world. But a slight introspection would reveal that at present the momentum seems to be losing its steam. The various corruption issues opening up like a can of worms is not only severely denting investor confidence, it has all the ammo to derail the much touted Indian growth story. The signs are ominous. FDI in India declined in this year. GDP growth is declining steadily to 7.7 per cent in the second quarter of 2011. Investors are holding up investments, capital is locked up in projects and negative signs post August/September 2010 is all encompassing. There is something in the air which is preventing any further movement, awaiting a big push for the return of the feel good factor. The mood is sombre, and the corporate earning figures have also not lifted up the spirit. Deep rooted corruption and total apathy of the common man in the system prevents an inclusive growth and is creating a bigger divide between the haves and the have nots which might result into India facing a Malthusian nightmare instead of reaping its demographic dividend.

The Government needs to get its act together and take some bold decisions to unshackle the system and induce further growth. The Government should make some bold announcements to convey its willingness to come clean on matters of corruption and black money. We need an out of the box approach to achieve this. The tax rates should be lowered significantly. Specific moves like zero capital gains tax and 1 per cent stamp duty on all real estate deals to encourage full value transactions is the need of the hour. Last time when we rationalised the tax system in 1985-86, all fears of loss of government revenue were put to rest when the actual tax collection was much higher by the lowering of taxes. We need a radical move from the government which dismantles the current rate provision.

Trust is a valuable social asset that forms the basis of democracy. Trust demands respect for the inherent value and rights of a human being. It is time for us to accept that while "taxes are the price we pay for civilization"– civilization cannot sustain itself without trust. Distrust kills transparency, creates divide and fuels manoeuvring to suit one's motive. If a government distrusts its people, people are likely to reciprocate by distrusting the system. Reciprocity and cooperation increase in a trust based regime where people trust that others will indeed reciprocate.

Sadly in India it is this trust that is missing. Recent events have only pointed out the extent of this trust deficit and the lack of faith that people have in the laid down processes and the norms of democracy that we so proudly hold to with high esteem. The best way to promote trust is to promote procedural justice, legitimacy and identification which would create a sense of respect for the authorities among the mass and a belief that he is being trusted by the men in power.

The government should encourage voluntary compliance. Forced compliance is leading to a situation where there is no fear of getting caught but, leading to an easier route of not complying and when the turn comes of being scrutinized, one easily gets away with payouts—invariably payouts are a cheaper option than compliance in monetary terms, wherein both parties benefit. The prevailing raid raj and high handedness of agencies aided by the discretionary power inbuilt in our laws is one of the key reasons for lack of compliance. Voluntary disclosure should be encouraged; instill trust in the system which would ultimately result in much greater compliance. It is not a novel idea, our previous experiences illustrate that a lower tax system accompanied by self-compliance will result into greater revenue collection, given our current improved e-governance. The developed countries in the world do not have the kind of a forced compliance that we have in India, but they have much better compliance. Hence it is high time we change the existing system which is corrupt and not working in our favour and announce some forward looking measures in this regard. Trust based compliance with strict enforcement in case of any breach of this trust is the need of the hour.

The Government should empower and encourage public participation in the cleansing process. Economic offenders should be made public and the highest tax payers should be honoured. Repeat offenders should pay steep and certain penalties and repeat performers should be awarded.

Our system provides overriding power to the enforcement agencies which leads to extortionary corruption. Policy correction can curb extortionary corruption. Moreover, it is extortionary corruption which affects the common man, the honest man. The tax laws should provide at least the minimum dignity to the taxpayers.

Trust based compliance with strict enforcement in case of any breach of this trust is the need of the hour. This would make the tax system more robust, transparent and vibrant. The call is for freedom from being harassed by the authorities due to the huge discretionary power that they enjoy. We may look at diluting this excessive discretionary power to enable more trust and faith in the system.

As a one time exercise, we may also look at an amnesty scheme to clear off all backlogs and post that treat whosoever evades tax with strict enforcement. The proposed amnesty scheme may be treated differently from all the previous amnesty schemes, since we did not have the kind of technology and e-governance previously that we have today. Today with the prevalent 360^0 profiling, we can literally track all transactions and expenditures of any individual, particularly of the high net worth individuals. The amnesty scheme would only help a large section of willing citizens to come clean and honest, who have been living in the muddle of corruption and deceit forced upon by the antediluvian tax system. Trust your citizen, and if he betrays your trust, punishment should be certain and exemplary.

Personally, I am against any amnesty scheme as it penalises the honest. A three year limitation for any investigation or enforcement, which itself would clear more than 80 per cent of the backlog in the system and divert all our resources to more recent ones to get results instead of motivated grave digging of evergreen cases without any convictions may be a better option. This would also free our citizens from a lifelong fear of the unknown, of being persecuted for things they may never have done or known and don't have enough time or money to fight the system in which they have been caught.

Today we need a bold message through action from the government that it intends to fight corruption and bring in transparency in governance. The government needs to walk the extra mile to announce some big ticket reforms to bring in some cheer in the investment climate. The present status quo needs to go and the country needs to start moving.

Do we really want to remove or reduce corruption?

Ensuring certainty of punishment rather than severity is the need of the hour, says Arun Kumar Jagatramka

The middle class - a broad canvas, that encompasses a huge section of our society, and is still, largely neglected by the development authorities. Neglected because they do not form a definite vote bank; a criterion which, unfortunately in our democracy determines the extent of political attention that one may command.

But in these recent years, the middle class has exhibited 'strength' and 'unity', and commanded attention, not only from the national government, but also from the world. Be it the demonstrations at Jantar Mantar or protests at India Gate against a barbaric act, the middle class's anger and intolerance to injustice has been evident. It would be naive to consider this anger as a one off event. Rather it is an outburst of a deeper anger, a manifestation against the depraved neglect and extortion of the vast middle class. This seething resentment is bound to explode again, at any instance of injustice which shakes the basic credo of being human and strikes a chord among the millions.

Extortion has been the bedrock of the present governance system in our country. It is universal, and all pervasive. Independent India has made huge progress. We have had an excellent economic growth. We have made remarkable advancement in science & technology, have been able to improve the living conditions of our people. But amidst all these achievements, we have also continued with the colonial legacy of extortion. As extortion thrived, corruption the direct by-product has also multiplied.

We take a myopic view of the system, introduce laws which encourage corruption and in the process hand out more tools for extortion. As an immediate example, recently a circular was issued by CBEC putting a deadline of 30 days for the taxpayers to obtain a stay against a disputed tax demand and allows the department officers to go for coercive recovery measures after 30 days irrespective of the merits of the case. The irony of the circular which abates extortion is that, even if the stay application is not heard for reasons attributable to the authorities themselves, the tax payer is at their mercy. Such draconian rules which are extortionary, certainly encourage corruption. Today all services except the 17 exempt heads under negative lists are covered under service tax net. This puts a vast array of people who would be subjected to extortion and thus increasing corruption in the country many fold. It is beyond the imagination of any right thinking individual that when there is a smouldering anger against extortion, when there is a raging debate on how to minimise corruption, how such regressive circulars & guidelines could be issued.

We need to follow the old maxim of "think before you act" and as such it also applies to the authorities in power before they promulgate any law. We have enough of laws. What we require is their correct implementation. Enacting harsh laws would not increase revenue collection. They only give a license to increase the payout. Instead we need to ensure 'certainty of punishment' to the criminal.

We talk of demographic dividend. But need to be careful of a Malthusian nightmare. It is time that we sit back and take serious note of things...

*The Economic Times—*28 January 2013

DO WE REALLY WANT TO REMOVE OR REDUCE CORRUPTION?

Ensuring certainty of punishment rather than severity is the need of the hour, says Arun Kumar Jagatramka

The middle class—a broad canvas, that encompasses a huge section of our society, and is still, largely neglected by the development authorities. Neglected because they do not form a definite vote bank; a criterion which, unfortunately in our democracy determines the extent of political attention that one may command.

But in these recent years, the middle class has exhibited 'strength' and 'unity' and commanded attention, not only from the national government, but also from the world. Be it the demonstrations at Jantar Mantar or protests at India Gate against a barbaric act, the middle class's anger and intolerance to injustice has been evident. It would be naïve to consider this anger as a one off event. Rather it is an outburst of a deeper anger, a manifestation against the depraved neglect and extortion of the vast middle class. This seething resentment is bound to explode again, at any instance of injustice which shakes the basic credo of being human and strikes a chord among the millions.

Extortion has been the bedrock of the present governance system in our country. It is universal, and all pervasive. Independent India has made huge progress. We have had an excellent economic growth. We have made remarkable advancement in science & technology, have been able to improve the living conditions of our people. But amidst all these achievements, we have also continued with the colonial legacy of extortion. As extortion thrived, corruption the direct by-product has also multiplied.

We take a myopic view of the system, introduce laws which encourage corruption and in the process hand out more tools for extortion. As an immediate example, recently a circular was issued by CBEC putting a deadline of 30 days for the taxpayers to obtain a stay against a disputed tax demand and allows the department officers to go for coercive recovery measures after 30 days irrespective of the merits of the case. The irony of the circular which abates extortion is that, even if the stay application is not heard for reasons attributable to the authorities themselves, the tax payer is at their mercy. Such draconian rules which are extortionary, certainly encourage corruption. Today all services except the 17 exempt heads under negative lists are covered under service tax net. This puts a vast array of people who would be subjected to extortion and thus increasing corruption in the country many fold. It is beyond the imagination of any right thinking individual that when there is a smouldering anger against extortion, when there is a raging debate on how to minimise corruption, how such regressive circulars & guidelines could be issued.

We need to follow the old maxim of "think before you act" and as such it also applies to the authorities in power before they promulgate any law. We have enough of laws. What we require is their correct implementation. Enacting harsh laws would not increase revenue collection. They only give a license to increase the payout. Instead we need to ensure 'certainty of punishment' to the criminal.

We talk of demographic dividend. But need to be careful of a Malthusian nightmare. It is time that we sit back and take serious note of things…

TOWARDS A PEOPLE-FRIENDLY GOVERNMENT
Ethical deficit to trust deficit — cushioning the social diseconomies

Arun Kumar Jagatramka
Chairman and Managing Director
Gujarat NRE Coke Ltd

The first and foremost expectation from the new government has already been achieved even without the first bullet being fired. The 'feel good factor' and reinstilling trust of the common man in the system has been achieved very successfully by Modiji even before he has taken oath as the Prime Minister of India. I am sure in the days to come concrete steps would be taken by the government to remove the trust deficit which has been corroding the fabric of the nation. Industry needs to be reassured that their investment is protected and that there would not be any retrospective

LARGE TAXPAYERS NEED TO BE HONOURED INSTEAD OF THE CURRENT MINDSET OF 'CATCH THE BIG FISH'. SEARCH AND SEIZURE SHOULD BE AN EXCEPTION AND NOT THE RULE

effect or revisiting an approval. The bureaucracy needs to be given a free hand in doing what is good for development and growth. At the same time, the guilty shall not go unpunished.

■ Removing the license raj - industry and bureaucracy, who have already been struggling to cope with a plethora of old regulations are today faced with an avalanche of new ones imposed on them in the last few years. The most onerous are related to the environment, forests, tribal areas, and land acquisition. These have created a new license-permit raj. Honest business has become impossible in several areas, notably natural resources and land. Dishonest business though is still possible through kickbacks. Need to create an enabling environment for honest business.

NEED TO CREATE AN ENABLING ENVIRONMENT FOR HONEST BUSINESS

■ Ease of doing business - Policies need to be simplified by simplifying the excessive regulations that bind us today. Do away with the discretionary powers that breed corruption.

Addressing the above issues would solve a host of problems including economic woes.

Boosting India's sluggish economy
The important issue that India Inc is waiting for the government to address is the slowdown in the economic activity in the country. Following are the certain measures that the new government may pursue:

■ Revival of Investment in infrastructure and manufacturing - Encourage investment in infrastructure and manufacturing. Review all the projects that are stuck at various stages to fast track their approval and monitor their progress at stages to expedite their completion. Revive the job scenario to create employment for educated youth and to take benefit of the demographic dividend.

■ Land acquisition and labour reforms - Though we have a new land acquisition policy, it is filled with conditions that make land acquisition much tougher. The government needs to review them and make land acquisition much easier without undermining the rights and benefits of the original land holders through an attractive R&R policy. The labour laws must be revisited to make them in accordance to

the market need. Today the tough regulations go on to protect the job, but the worker sadly is less protected which needs to be changed. Progressive labour laws would increase more job opportunities in the market.

Fiscal reforms
The entire tax structure - both direct (personal and corporate income tax) and indirect - needs a change for the better.

■ Simplification of tax laws.

■ Introduction of goods & services tax (GST) at the earliest without any further delay.

■ Introduction of Direct Tax Code (DTC) after suitable modifications.

A check on discretionary powers and much higher level of accountability of the revenue officials is the need of the hour. The revenue officials need to overhaul their mindset that the taxpayer is paying for their livelihood as well and is not to be treated as a criminal but deserves respect. Large taxpayers need to be honoured instead of the current mindset of 'Catch the big fish'. Search and seizure should be an exception and not the rule.

Legal reforms
The legal reforms include a whole gamut of changes primary among them is the removal of obsolete and antiquated laws. Any law that cannot be complied by most citizens should be scrapped. We do not need to formulate any new law/regulation, we just need to simplify the existing and focus on its implementation. Implementation should be based on the principle of certainty of punishment rather than its severity.

PROGRESSIVE LABOUR LAWS WOULD CREATE MORE JOB OPPORTUNITIES IN THE MARKET

Attention is also required in removing confusions with regards to the Companies Act. The Companies Act, 2013, replaces the old law with nearly 700 conflicting sections with 470 sections. However, a modern law does not by itself become a great law, for its success depends on how smoothly it can be implemented which is certainly missing in the new Act and hence needs an urgent review.

IMPLEMENTATION SHOULD BE BASED ON THE PRINCIPLE OF CERTAINTY OF PUNISHMENT RATHER THAN ITS SEVERITY

Administrative reforms
In the administrative front certain reforms have become utmost important. These include:

■ Modernize the police and insulate them from political influence - **police reforms.**

■ Enact public grievance redressal bill.

■ Ensure trust-based compliance instead of regular harassment by enforcement agencies.

Judicial reforms
An independent and impartial judiciary and a speedy and efficient system are the very essence of civilization. However, our judiciary, by its very nature, has become ponderous, excruciatingly slow and inefficient. This alarming situation calls for speedy remedial reforms. These measures should be practical and effective while they are in consonance with the basic features of the Constitution. They include:

■ Improvement in the judge - population ratio.

■ Enact laws on judicial appointments and accountability.

■ Fast track resolution of pending cases - **justice delayed is justice denied.**

For efficient and transparent functioning of the government the following measures are a must:

■ Bring about an end to wasteful government expenditure.

■ Ensure allocation of natural resources in a transparent manner through auctions.

■ Government should progressively come out from being the majority owner of natural resources and encourage more private investment to bring in efficiency and productivity through use of technology. Government's role should be to monitor that such activity is within the prescribed environment and safety norms and strict action may be taken for any violation.

The Economic Times—26 May 2014

TOWARDS A PEOPLE-FRIENDLY GOVERNMENT
*Ethical deficit to trust deficit–cushioning
the social diseconomies*

The first and foremost expectation from the new government has already been achieved even without the first bullet being fired. The 'feel good factor' and reinstilling trust of the common man in the system has been achieved very successfully by Modiji even before he has taken oath as the Prime Minister of India. I am sure in the days to come concrete steps would be taken by the government to remove the trust deficit which has been corroding the fabric of the nation. Industry needs to be reassured that their investment is protected and that there would not be any retrospective effect or revisiting an approval. The bureaucracy needs to be given a free hand in doing what is good for development and growth. At the same time, the guilty shall not go unpunished.

LARGE TAXPAYERS NEED TO BE HONOURED INSTEAD OF THE CURRENT MINDSET OF 'CATCH THE BIG FISH'. SEARCH AND SEIZURE SHOULD BE AN EXCEPTION AND NOT THE RULE

- Removing the license raj—industry and bureaucracy, who have already been struggling to cope with a plethora of old regulations are today faced with an avalanche of new ones imposed on them in the last few years. The most onerous are related to the environment, forests, tribal areas, and land acquisition. These have created a new license-permit raj. Honest business has become impossible in several areas, notably natural resources and land. Dishonest business though is still possible through kickbacks. Need to create an enabling environment for honest business.

NEED TO CREATE AN ENABLING ENVIRONMENT FOR HONEST BUSINESS

- Ease of doing business—Policies need to be simplified by simplifying the excessive regulations that bind us today. Do away with the discretionary powers that bred corruption.
  Addressing the above issues would solve a host of problems including economic woes.

Boosting India's sluggish economy

The important issue that India Inc is waiting for the government to address is the slowdown in the economic activity in the country. Following are the certain measures that the new government may pursue:

- Revival of Investment in Infrastructure and manufacturing—Encourage investment in infrastructure and manufacturing. Review all the projects that are stuck at various stages to fast track their approval and monitor their progress at stages to expedite their completion. Revive the job scenario to create employment for educated youth and to take benefit of the demographic dividend.
- Land acquisition and labour reforms—Though we have a new land acquisition policy, it is filled with conditions that make land acquisition much tougher. The government needs to review them and make land acquisition much easier without undermining the rights and benefits of the original land holders through an attractive R&R policy. The labour laws must be revisited to make them in accordance to the market need. Today the tough regulations go on to protect the job, but the worker sadly is less protected which needs to be changed. Progressive labour laws would increase more job opportunities in the market.

Fiscal reforms

The entire tax structure—both direct (personal and corporate income tax) and indirect—needs a change for the better.

- Simplification of tax laws.
- Introduction of goods & services tax (GST) at the earliest without any further delay.
- Introduction of Direct Tax Code (DTC) after suitable modifications.

A check on discretionary powers and much higher level of accountability of the revenue officials is the need of the hour. The revenue officials need to overhaul their mindset that the taxpayer is paying for their livelihood as well and is not to be treated as a criminal but deserves respect.

Large taxpayers need to be honoured instead of the current mindset of

'Catch the big fish'. Search and seizure should be an exception and not the rule.

Legal reforms

The legal reforms include a whole gamut of changes primary among them is the removal of obsolete and antiquated laws. Any law that cannot be complied by most citizens should be scrapped. We do not need to formulate any new law/regulation, we just need to simplify the existing and focus on its implementation. Implementation should be based on the principle of certainty of punishment rather than its severity.

PROGRESSIVE LABOUR LAWS WOULD CREATE MORE JOB OPPORTUNITIES IN THE MARKET

Attention is also required in removing confusions with regards to the Companies Act. The Companies Act 2013, replaces the old law with nearly 700 conflicting sections with 470 sections. However, a modern law does not by itself become a great law, for its success depends on how smoothly it can be implemented which is certainly missing in the new Act and hence needs an urgent review.

IMPLEMENTION SHOULD BE BASED ON THE PRINCIPLE OF CERTAINTY OF PUNISHMENT RATHER THAN ITS SEVERITY

Administrative reforms

In the administrative front certain reforms have become utmost important. These include:

- Modernize the police and insulate them from political influence—**police reforms**.
- Enact public grievance redressal bill.
- Ensure trust-based compliance instead of regular harassment by enforcement agencies.

Judicial reforms

An independent and impartial judiciary and a speedy and efficient system are the very essence of civilization. However, our judiciary, by its very nature, has become ponderous, excruciatingly slow and inefficient. This alarming situation calls for speedy remedial reforms. These measures should be practical and effective while they are in consonance with the basic features of the Constitution. They include:

- Improvement in the judge-population ratio.
- Enact laws on judicial appointments and accountability.
- Fast track resolution of pending cases—**justice delayed is justice denied**.

For efficient and transparent functioning of the government the following measures are a must :

- Bring about an end to wasteful government expenditure.
- Ensure allocation of natural resources in a transparent manner through auctions.
- Government should progressively come out from being the majority owner of natural resources and encourage more private investment to bring in efficiency and productivity through use of technology. Government's role should be to monitor that such activity is within the prescribed environment and safety norms and strict action may be taken for any violation.

CERTAINTY MATTERS

An insight into the need for certainty of punishment rather than its severity

ARUN KUMAR JAGATRAMKA
CHAIRMAN AND MANAGING DIRECTOR
GUJARAT NRE COKE LTD

Compliance with laws and regulations depend on the expected penalty facing the violators. The expected penalty, in turn, depends on both the probability of the certainty of punishment and the severity of the punishment, if caught. For a country like India, where anything and every-

Implementation should be based on the principle of certainty of punishment rather than its severity

thing is possible with a little bit of greasing the palm, the probability of the certainty of punishment has tended to go down day by day. Criminals are not deterred by the severity of the sentence but by the certainty of punishment, and given the 'chalta hai' attitude governing the largest democracy of the world, India flourishes to be a heaven of the law-breakers.

Governance and the judicial system are on the verge of being collapsed in India. Cases that should be disposed off in three months are pending for thirteen years. The system has degenerated to such an extent that no one can touch you if you have the right

Enhancing the severity of punishment will have little impact on people who do not believe they will be apprehended for their actions, as in the case of India

connections. In such a scenario, harshness of laws is not the solution as you are not likely to be caught; rather, the stress should be on enforcing the swiftness and inevitability of justice. Evidence has shown that certainty of punishment is more effective than tougher sentences.

The main problem lies with the fact that the obsolete and antiqued laws of the land are too complex to be interpreted in their right spirit and needs

simplification. Any law that cannot be complied by most of the citizens must be scrapped. The stress should be on the implementation thereby ensuring certainty of punishment. Firstly, by increasing the certainty of punishment, potential offenders may be deterred by the risk of apprehension. For example, if there is an increase in the number of mobile police van patrolling, some drivers may stop ignoring red lights in order to get caught for breaking the law. Secondly, the severity of punishment may influence behaviour

The obsolete and antiqued laws of the land are too complex to be interpreted in their right spirit and needs simplification

of individuals if potential offenders weigh the consequences of their actions and conclude that the risks of punishment are too severe.

If there was cent percent certainty of being apprehended for committing a crime, few people would do so. But since most crimes, including serious ones, do not result in an arrest and conviction, the overall deterrent effect of the certainty of punishment is substantially reduced. Clearly, enhancing the severity of punishment will have little impact on people who do not believe they will be apprehended for their actions, as in the case of India. There must be zero tolerance for breaking the law in India. The solution lies in the effective system to apprehend the perpetrators and effective prosecution so that no one escapes from the hands of law. Reforms to ensure the above should be immediately implemented by the government.

The Economic Times—24 July 2014

CERTAINTY MATTERS

An insight into the need for certainty of punishment rather than its severity

Compliance with laws and regulations depends on the expected penalty facing the violators. The expected penalty, in turn, depends on both the probability of the certainty of punishment and the severity of the punishment, if caught. For a country like India, where anything and everything is possible with a little bit of greasing the palm, the probability of the certainty of punishment has tended to go down day by day. **Criminals are not deterred by the severity of the sentence but by the certainty of punishment, and given the '*chalta hai*' attitude governing the largest democracy of the world, India flourishes to be a heaven of the law-breakers.**

IMPLEMENTATION SHOULD BE BASED ON THE PRINCIPLE OF CERTAINTY OF PUNISHMENT RATHER THAN ITS SEVERITY

Governance and the judicial system are on the verge of being collapsed in India. Cases that should be disposed off [*sic*] in three months are pending for thirteen years. The system has degenerated to such an extent that no one can touch you if you have the right connections. In such a scenario, harshness of laws is not the solution as you are not likely to be caught; rather, the stress should be on enforcing the swiftness and inevitability of justice. Evidence has shown that certainty of punishment is more effective than tougher sentences.

ENHANCING THE SEVERITY OF PUNISHMENT WILL HAVE LITTLE IMPACT ON PEOPLE WHO DO NOT BELIEVE THEY WILL BE APPREHENDED FOR THEIR ACTIONS, AS IN THE CASE OF INDIA

The main problem lies with the fact that the obsolete and antiqued laws of the land are too complex to be interpreted in their right spirit and needs simplification. Any law that cannot be complied by most of the citizens must be scrapped. The stress should be on the implementation thereby ensuring certainty of punishment. Firstly, by increasing the certainty of punishment, potential offenders may be deterred by the risk of apprehension. For example, if there is an increase in the number of mobile police van patrolling, some drivers may stop ignoring red lights in order to get caught for breaking the law. Secondly, the severity of punishment may influence behaviour of individuals if potential offenders weigh the consequences of their actions and conclude that the risks of punishment are too severe.

THE OBSOLETE AND ANTIQUED LAWS OF THE LAND ARE TOO COMPLEX TO BE INTERPRETED IN THEIR RIGHT SPIRIT AND NEEDS SIMPLIFICATION

If there was cent percent certainty of being apprehended for committing a crime, few people would do so. But since most crimes, including serious ones, do not result in an arrest and conviction, the overall deterrent effect of the certainty of punishment is substantially reduced. Clearly, enhancing the severity of punishment will have little impact on people who do not believe they will be apprehended for their actions, as in the case of India. There must be zero tolerance for breaking the law in India. The solution lies in the effective system to apprehend the perpetrators and effective prosecution so that no one escapes from the hands of law. Reforms to ensure the above should be immediately implemented by the government.

THE ECONOMIC TIMES, KOLKATA, WEDNESDAY, 27 AUGUST 2014

Tax Terrorism: The Terror Within

There must be a system where the government honours the large tax-payers to encourage voluntary tax compliance

ARUN KUMAR JAGATRAMKA
CHAIRMAN AND MANAGING DIRECTOR
GUJARAT NRE COKE LTD

Though we are quite familiar with the phase 'terrorism tax' wherein tax collected from the people is used to fight terrorist activities, yet the term 'tax terrorism' seems to have hit the headlines recently. It was first traced in the comments of our Prime Minister, Sri Narendra Modi, at an industry interaction wherein he stated the need to end it. This phrase has gained wide spread acceptability and support in the past few months.

Tax reforms, as most of us accept, is the need of the hour. But before one embarks on this tedious journey of correcting the 'bad' laws, it would be wiser to first deal with tax terrorism. For a layman, this term implies a situation where the taxman uses his powers to extract more tax than is due from an honest tax-payer. This may be either in the form of unjust and inequitable tax laws or by enforcing the tax law on the general public in a harsh manner,

Tax reforms is the need of the hour. But before correcting the 'bad laws', one should tackle tax terrorism

which generally happens when the taxman views every transaction with suspect.

Over the past few years, the Income Tax department has come under severe criticism from all quarters for its aggressive attitude in not only enforcing the law, but also in formulating ridiculous strategies like 'catch the big fish'. There have also been several cases that have been handled in a very unprecedented and unprofessional manner.

If we do an impartial study of the tax laws, we find that the government has

not done any terrorism by introducing new laws aimed at curbing tax avoidance. The laws that have been introduced are in accordance with international anti-corruption and anti-avoidance measures. Barring aside a few policy initiatives, none of the recent changes can be termed as anything near to tax terrorism.

However, when we observe the ways and means of enforcement of these laws, tax terrorism looms large. Take the following example. A few years back, the then highest tax paying Bollywood actress gets hounded by taxmen at 7 am in the morning. The 'masala' story making rounds in the newspapers and Page 3 circles was the

Tax terrorism lies not in policy formulation but in the enforcement

presence of a Bollywood actor in her house at that odd hour. Nobody, however, questioned why the tax officials went to her place at 7 am in the morning? The exponential increase in disputes related to the transfer pricing regulations is another apt example of tax terrorism. It has generally been felt by the taxman that whoever is covered by these regulations must have employed some evasionary or tax avoidance techniques in business, hence, this humungous increase in the number of cases.

Tax terrorism lies not in policy formulation but in the enforcement. The concept of enforcement has been overlooked till date and should not be neglected any further. Reforms have become imminent in the enforcement process in a manner so that the taxman appreciates the commercial principles behind business and search and seizure doesn't become a general rule.

Honouring the large tax-payers will infuse a sense of encouragement among the people; they will feel that the government is people-friendly

In fact, there should be a system where the government should encourage voluntary tax compliance in terms of honouring the large tax-payers. This will infuse a sense of encouragement among the people; they will feel that the government is people-friendly rather than people-evasive.

The government must initiate actions which make it clear that the Indian taxman is equipped with the necessary knowledge of when to use the law and not a 'tax terrorist' who indiscriminately uses the tax laws to cause discontent.

The Economic Times—27 August 2014

TAX TERRORISM: THE TERROR WITHIN

*There must be a system where the government honours the large tax-payers
to encourage voluntary tax compliance*

Though we are quite familiar with the phase 'terrorism tax' wherein tax collected from the people is used to fight terrorist activities, yet the term 'tax terrorism' seems to have hit the headlines recently. It was first traced in the comments of our Prime Minister, Sri Narendra Modi, at an industry interaction wherein he stated the need to end it. This phrase has gained widespread acceptability and support in the past few months.

Tax reforms, as most of us accept, is the need of the hour. But before one embarks on this tedious journey of correcting the "bad" laws, it would be wiser to first deal with tax terrorism. For a layman, this term implies a situation where the taxman uses his powers to extract more tax than is due from an honest tax-payer. This may be either in the form of unjust and inequitable tax laws or by enforcing the tax law on the general public in a harsh manner, which generally happens when the taxman views every transaction with suspect.

TAX REFORMS IS THE NEED OF THE HOUR. BUT BEFORE CORRECTING THE 'BAD LAWS, ONE SHOULD TACKLE TAX TERRORISM

Over the past few years, the Income Tax department has come under severe criticism from all quarters for its aggressive attitude in not only enforcing the law, but also in formulating ridiculous strategies like 'catch the big fish'. There have also been several cases that have been several cases that have been handled in a very unprecedented and unprofessional manner.

If we do an impartial study of the tax laws, we find that the government has not done any terrorism by introducing new laws aimed at curbing tax avoidance. The laws that have been introduced are in accordance with international anti-corruption and anti-avoidance measures. Barring aside a few policy initiatives, none of the recent changes can be termed as anything near to tax terrorism.

However, when we observe the ways and means of enforcement of these laws, tax terrorism looms large. Take the following example. A few years back, the then highest tax paying Bollywood actress gets hounded by taxmen at 7 am in the morning. The 'masala' story making rounds in the newspaper and Page 3 circles was the presence of a Bollywood actor in her house at that odd hour. Nobody, however, questioned why the tax officials went to her place at 7 am in the morning? The exponential increase in disputes related to the transfer pricing regulations is another apt example of tax terrorism. It has generally been felt by the taxman that whoever is covered by these regulations must have employed some evasionary of tax avoidance techniques in business, hence, this humungous increase in the number of cases.

Tax terrorism lies not in policy formulation but in the enforcement. The concept of enforcement has been overlooked till date and should not be neglected any further. Reforms have become imminent in the enforcement process in a manner so that the taxman appreciates the commercial principles behind business and search and seizure doesn't become a general rule.

HONOURING THE LARGE TAX-PAYERS WILL INFUSE A SENSE OF ENCOURAGEMENT AMONG THE PEOPLE; THEY WILL FEEL THAT THE GOVERNMENT IS PEOPLE-FRIENDLY

In fact, there should be a system where the government should encourage voluntary tax compliance in terms of honouring the large tax-payers. This will infuse a sense of encouragement among the people; they will feel that the government is people-friendly rather than people-evasive.

The government must initiate actions which make it clear that the Indian taxman is equipped with the necessary knowledge of when to use the law and not a 'tax terrorist' who indiscriminately uses the tax laws to cause discontent.

CLEAN THY COAL

Certainty of punishment can be the only way to stop flourishing corruption

ARUN KUMAR JAGATRAMKA
CHAIRMAN AND MANAGING DIRECTOR
GUJARAT NRE COKE LTD

Coal has long been the face of thriving corruption in India both as a means as well as an end in itself. Indian Coal economy has been a victim of the 'vice of arbitrariness and legal flaws' as the Honourable Court has put it. The recent Supreme Court decision terming all coal block allocations between 1993 and 2010 as 'illegal' should be taken as an opportunity and a blessing in disguise by the industry and the government alike to clean up the mess.

The government has rightly not opposed the deallocation of all the coal blocks. All the 218 mines allocated during the period, whose allocation process has been questioned by the Supreme Court should be deallocated. Any move to save any mine from deallocation would be counterproductive. The price attached to deallocation of producing mines would be a price well paid, for the growth of the coal economy and various industries dependent on coal as well as a shot in the arm for the bigger war against corruption.

Moreover, the companies that have been allotted mines have already made windfall gains through access to cheap resources for so long. Deallocation of coal mines is not new and there are examples of deallocation of mines on charges of corruption in other countries as well. The government of New South Wales, Australia had in the past supported the recommendations made by the corruption watchdog Independent Commission against Corruption (ICAC) into how coal mining licenses are managed across the state leading to cancellation of coal licences. The opaque coal economy would get an opportunity to be transparent and conducive for growth on similar lines in India.

The Indian industry should also support this deallocation, since it would present an opportunity to start with a clean slate. For long the corporate sector in India has been not so vocal against corruption. Corruption though affects the majority in industry; a handful finds it convenient to bend the system in their favour to mint money. This has flourished due to absence of certainty of punishment. One who benefits from this collusive corruption wants the status quo to remain. The guilty needs to be punished and we need to have certainty of punishment to arrest the loot.

The observation of the apex court indeed calls for certainty of

The price attached to deallocation of producing mines would be a price well-paid for the growth of the coal economy and various industries dependent on coal as well as a shot in the arm for the bigger war against corruption

punishment. India has the third largest reserves of coal. But the irony lies that we are one of the largest importers of coal and would shortly overtake China to become the largest importer in the world. The fallacy lies in our coal policy which requires a complete overhaul. I am confident that the new government through its dynamic leadership would be able to put the systems in place.

A pragmatic coal policy is vital for the country's economy as coal forms the backbone of two critical industries, namely power and steel. A vibrant power sector and a dynamic steel industry are vital to fuel India's industrialisation and in fulfilling the "Make in India" mission of our Prime Minister.

It would be wrong to blame Coal India for India's low coal production. One company cannot meet the burgeoning demand of a growing economy. The fault is in the "ill-conceived" Coal Mines Nationalisation Act. The Act, at the time of its formulation, did help in consolidation of small unorganised mines into a single entity, thereby increasing safety parameters, safe-guarding the miners, stopping rampant illegal mining and making coal mining an organised industry. However, on realising the pitfalls of this Act - that comes in the way of increasing production in sync with demand, we took the easier route of bypassing it by introducing captive mining concept.

The concept of captive mining is laced with an undue benefit to the captive user, as the allottee gets access to coal at a much cheaper rate than the market rate. The allottee of captive mine is thus at a more advantageous position compared to its peer in the industry and it defeats the concept of level playing field which the government should always present unbiased to all industries. Irrespective of the process of allotment that is followed, the captive policy also does not solve the problem of increasing production. The captive miners though sitting on coal reserves more than their requirement were constrained to not sell coal to the market which continues to starve of this resource and is forced to import. The pitfall of importing is not restricted to the importing company but also to the general economy which is known to all. To add to this, captive mining had led to the development of small and fragmented mines that have not been able to enjoy the economies of scale.

Furthermore, process industries may not have the expertise in mining and it should be left to mining companies that excel in this field to ensure that the nation gets full benefits of its vast mineral resources.

The time has come for which the

A vibrant power sector and a dynamic steel industry are vital to fuel India's industrialisation and in fulfilling the mission of 'Make in India'

Supreme Court has already set the ball rolling, to remove the concept of captive mining and to introduce private mining for commercial purpose. We should identify mines, have all the clearances in place and privatise them through an open and transparent auction. Private miners should be allowed to sell coal openly to the market which would in itself increase India's coal production many folds and we would be able to meet our demand for power industry through domestic resource.

An independent regulator may be brought in to oversee and check any violation. Any violation should be dealt with certainty of punishment within a stipulated time frame. We should not miss this opportunity to open up coal sector in India, increase our coal production and most important, rid it of crony capitalism by bringing in transparency.

The Economic Times—17 September 2014

CLEAN THY COAL

Certainty of punishment can be the only way to stop flourishing corruption

Coal has long been the face of thriving corruption in India both as a means as well as an end in itself. Indian Coal economy has been a victim of the 'vice of arbitrariness and legal flaws' as the Honourable Court has put it. The recent Supreme Court decision terming all coal block allocations between 1993 and 2010 as 'illegal' should be taken as an opportunity and a blessing in disguise by the industry and the government alike to clean up the mess.

The government has rightly not opposed the deallocation of all the coal blocks. All the 218 mines allocated during the period, whose allocation process has been questioned by the Supreme Court should be deallocated. Any move to save any mine from deallocation would be counterproductive. The price attached to deallocation of producing mines would be a price well paid, for the growth of the coal economy and various industries dependent on coal as well as a shot in the arm for the bigger war against corruption.

Moreover, the companies that have been allotted mines have already made windfall gains through access to cheap resources for so long. Deallocation of coal mines is not new and there are examples of deallocation of mines on charges of corruption in other countries as well. The government of New South Wales, Australia had in the past supported the recommendations made by the corruption watchdog Independent Commission against Corruption (ICAC) into how coal mining licenses are managed across the state leading to cancellation of coal licences. The opaque coal economy would get an opportunity to be transparent and conducive for growth on similar lines in India.

The Indian industry should also support this deallocation, since it would present an opportunity to start with a clean state. For long the corporate sector in India has been not so vocal against corruption. Corruption though affects the majority in industry: a handful finds it convenient to bend the system in their favour to mint money. This has flourished due to absence of certainty of punishment. One who benefits from this collusive corruption wants the status quo to remain. The guilty needs to be punished and we need to have certainty of punishment to arrest the loot.

The observation of the apex court indeed calls for certainty of punishment. India has the third largest reserves of coal. But the irony lies that we are one of the largest importers of coal and would shortly overtake China to become the largest importer in the world. The fallacy lies in our coal policy which requires a complete overhaul. I am confident that the new government through its dynamic leadership would be able to put the systems in place.

THE PRICE ATTACHED TO DEALLOCATION OF PRODUCING MINES WOULD BE A PRICE WELL-PAID FOR THE GROWTH OF THE COAL ECONOMY AND VARIOUS INDUSTRIES DEPENDENT ON COAL AS WELL AS A SHORT IN THE ARM FOR THE BIGGER WAR AGAINST CORRUPTION

A pragmatic coal policy is vital for the country's economy as coal forms the backbone of two critical industries, namely power and steel. A vibrant power sector and a dynamic steel industry are vital to fuel India's industrialisation and in fulfilling the "Make in India" mission of our Prime Minister.

It would be wrong to blame Coal India for India's low coal production. One company cannot meet the burgeoning demand of a growing economy. The fault is in the "ill-conceived" Coal Mines Nationalisation Act. The Act, at the time of its formulation, did help in consolidation of small unorganised mines into a single entity, thereby increasing safety parameters, safe-guarding the miners, stopping rampant illegal mining and making coal mining an organised industry. However, on realising the pitfalls of this Act—that comes in the way of increasing production in sync with demand, we took the easier route of bypassing it by introducing captive mining concept.

The concept of captive mining is laced with an undue benefit to the captive user, as the allottee gets access to coal at a much cheaper rate than the market rate. The allottee of captive mine is thus at a more advantageous position compared to its peer in the industry and it defeats the concept of level playing field which the government should always present unbiased to all industries. Irrespective of the process of allotment that is followed, the captive policy also does not solve the problem of increasing production. The captive miners though sitting on coal reserves more than their requirement were constrained to not sell coal to the market which continues to starve of this resource and is forced to import. The pitfall of importing is not restricted to the importing company but also to the general economy which is known to all. To add to this, captive mining had led to the development of small and fragmented mines that have not been able to enjoy the economies of scale.

Furthermore, process industries may not have the expertise in mining and it should be left to mining companies that excel in this field to ensure that the nation gets full benefits of its vast mineral resources.

The time has come for which the Supreme Court has already set the ball rolling, to remove the concept of captive mining and to introduce private mining for commercial purpose. We should identify mines, have all the clearances in place and privatise them through an open and transparent auction. Private miners should be allowed to sell coal openly to the market which would in itself increase India's coal production many folds and we would be able to meet our demand for power industry through domestic resource.

A VIBRANT POWER SECTOR AND A DYNAMIC STEEL INDUSTRY ARE VITAL TO FUEL INDIA'S INDUSTRIALISATION AND IN FULFILLING THE MISSION OF 'MAKE IN INDIA'

An independent regulator may be brought in to oversee and check any violation. Any violation should be dealt with certainty of punishment within a stipulated time frame. We should not miss this opportunity to open up coal sector in India, increase our coal production and most important, rid it of crony capitalism by bringing in transparency.

WWW.ECONOMICTIMES.COM

ADVERTORIAL

NPA RESOLUTION THROUGH LIQUIDATION?

LIQUIDATION AS A RESOLUTION TO NPA CRISIS WOULD BE DISASTROUS FOR THE ECONOMY, SOCIETY AND THE BANKING SYSTEM

ARUN KUMAR JAGATRAMKA
chairman and managing director
Gujarat NRE Coke Ltd & chairman,
Assocham National Council on Ease of
Doing Business

> BANKS ARE NOT EXPECTED TO CLOSE THE ECONOMY. INDIA IS NOT CLOSING AND NEEDS ITS INDUSTRIES FOR ITS PEOPLE. WASHING OFF ITS HAND FROM THE STRESSED ASSETS AT PALTRY LIQUIDATION VALUE IS IN EFFECT DESTRUCTION OF ASSETS. SUCH AN APPROACH OF BANKS WOULD RESULT IN HUGE JOB LOSSES AND UNEMPLOYMENT WOULD RISE MULTIFOLD. LIQUIDATION OF COMPANIES AT SCRAP VALUE BY THE BANKS, EVEN IF THE COMPANIES ARE IN PRODUCTION, MAKING PROFIT, PROVIDING EMPLOYMENT TO A FEW THOUSAND PEOPLE, CONTRIBUTING TO THE GOVERNMENT EXCHEQUER BY MAKING ALL TAX AND STATUTORY PAYMENTS ON TIME, WOULD BE DETRIMENTAL TO THE INDUSTRIAL SCENARIO AND SOCIO-ECONOMIC LANDSCAPE OF THE COUNTRY

The approach in IB Code should have been different. It should have started with two basic questions:

>> Is the company viable?
>> What is the sustainable debt based on independent study?

CDR AS A RESOLUTION MECHANISM FAILED BECAUSE...

>> Restructuring was often done just to delay the classification of an account as NPA rather than making efforts to make it viable

>> The interest of banks was in maintaining the account as standard instead of ensuring revival and sustainable operations

>> There was no effort on the part of the banks to identify the reasons for sickness and to address them

>> The effect of downturn in external environment was often ignored

>> Banks were under a wish list syndrome in suggesting models that would be acceptable to their sanctioning authority with an eye on provisioning and NPA management, without considering viability

The Economic Times—16 January 2018

NPA RESOLUTION THROUGH LIQUIDATION?
Liquidation as a Resolution to NPA Crisis would be Disastrous for the Economy, Society and the Banking System

Today, the Indian Industry is reeling under a severe debt trap. The long list of companies that are being referred to the National Company Law Tribunal (NCLT) under the Insolvency and Bankruptcy Code (IB Code), 2016 for Corporate Insolvency Resolution Process (CIRP) suggests that the cause for this huge debt is not only attributable to the individual companies but it is a mix of various external factors that have led to such debt crisis. The situation is complex and cannot be solved through the 'one size fits all' approach or through a cosmetic surgery. The cause of the bad loan needs to be ascertained to arrive at the solution that needs to be administered.

The reasons for the NPA crisis are a mix of various factors ranging from economic factors to companies overleveraging themselves with an obsession of growth and profit, and absence of a timely resolution in the banking system, resulting in the debts ballooning to an out of proportion limit today. The continued sluggishness in domestic growth for around a decade and slow recovery in the global economy have resulted in many projections going wrong.

Of course, like elsewhere, there are black sheep here as well but they can be identified through existing mechanism of forensic audits/wilful defaults etc and needs to be tackled separately. But the entire industry should not be treated in the same manner.

While everyone acknowledges and are in agreement with the reasons for the debt crisis, we have failed to find a practical solution to the problem.

Perhaps we are targeting at the wrong end towards mitigating the crisis. Through IB Code is a pragmatic process, however in our delivery mechanism, we are still following the same mistakes committed during the CDR regime.

The current ballooning NPA crisis could have been tackled long ago during 2012/2013, when a surge in the number of cases being referred to the CDR cell was noticed. However, instead of tackling it pragmatically when it first appeared, we preferred procrastination.

Over the last three to five years, we tried to manage NPA provisioning with an eye on banks' balance sheets instead of resolving the same through revival.

IB Code was introduced to find a commercially viable solution to the NPA crisis which could not be solved by various previous schemes like SDR, S4A, 5:25, etc. It promised to be a practical approach to arrive at a resolution of the corporate debt in the best interest of all the stakeholders. IB Code had superseded all the debt resolution mechanisms and was expected to correct the various shortcomings in the previous approaches.

However, IB Code in practice continues to harbour the ills of the previous processes. Lending is a commercial decision of the banks on which they earn interest and the borrower uses for investment for future returns.

BANKS ARE NOT EXPECTED TO CLOSE THE ECONOMY. INDIA IS NOT CLOSING AND NEEDS ITS INDUSTRIES FOR ITS PEOPLE. WASHING OFF ITS HAND FROM THE STRESSED ASSETS AT PALTRY LIQUIDATION VALUE IS IN EFFECT DESTRUCTION OF ASSETS. SUCH AN APPROACH OF BANKS WOULD RESULT IN HUGE JOB LOSSES AND UNEMPLOYMENT WOULD RISE MULTIFOLD. LIQUIDATION OF COMPANIES AT SCRAP VALUE BY THE BANKS, EVEN IF THE COMPANIES ARE IN PRODUCTION, MAKING PROFIT, PROVIDING EMPLOYMENT TO A FEW THOUSAND PEOPLE, CONTRIBUTING TO THE GOVERNMENT EXCHEQUER BY MAKING ALL TAX AND STATUTORY PAYMENTS ON TIME, WOULD BE DETRIMENTAL TO THE INDUSTRIAL SCENARIO AND SOCIO-ECONOMIC LANDSCAPE OF THE COUNTRY.

UNFORTUNATELY, IB CODE IN ITS CURRENT FORM SUPPORTS THE DECISION OF LENDERS TO LEND BUT PUNISHES THE DECISION OF THE BORROWERS TO BORROW WHEN THE LOAN TURNS BAD DUE TO REASONS BEYOND THE CONTROL OF BOTH.

The prime issue lies in our approach to solve the crisis. In all resolution mechanisms we start with the amount of debt and then try to negotiate on the wish lists for arriving at the minimum haircut and accordingly the sustainable debt without due consideration on its viability. The approach in IB Code should have been different. It should have started with two basic questions:

- Is the company viable?
- What is the sustainable debt based on independent study?

A company is considered to be viable if it can earn profit on its own strength. A Techno Economic Viability (TEV) study can bring out the quantum of income the company can have on a sustained basis.

Lenders have the right to demand their money while the borrowers are bound to pay the amount borrowed. However, that should not result into any mental block in the quantum of loan to be assigned as sustainable debt to arrive at the resolution. This should be purely based on the independent studies done dispassionately. The unsustainable portion can always be made up by assigning equity, zero coupon bonds, etc to the lenders. **As the company revives, the lenders can benefit from the upside of the equity. But in the tug of war between sustainable and unsustainable debt, the company may slip into liquidation where no one gains resulting into huge socio-economic collateral damage.**

The IB Code has vested enormous power on the secured creditors. The secured creditors through the committee of creditors (CoC) have been empowered to finalise the plan for revival of the company. This has been rightly done because it is the debt whose resolution is being done and the secured creditors are the best people to decide on the contours of doing so. However, with the rights, there should also be accountability on the CoC to ensure resolution.

Despite CIRP being a judicial process, banks are loath to take any decision on the resolution plans of the companies in insolvency. **Banks are afraid of enquiry by vigilance agencies of their decision on resolution plan and hence prefer procrastination, thus wasting valuable time.** There is no scope of inaction or indecisiveness under IB Code 2016. Indecisiveness or inaction in this time-bound process would only result into liquidation of productive assets along with its huge social and economic costs.

Banks are still in the wish list syndrome even under IB Code. They prefer to push companies in liquidation rather than taking a commercial decision of resolution even if the Net Asset Value (NAV) of the resolution plan is much higher than the liquidation value. Banks feel that they would be questioned on haircuts in resolution plan, while no questions would be asked to them in liquidation irrespective of how paltry the value that liquidation might fetch. Lenders are not interested in pursuing a resolution plan even if it does not require any fresh exposure and is based on internal accruals. Such obsession to liquidate productive assets ignoring the multiple times of higher Net Present Value (NPV) in resolution, defeats the basic idea of Corporate Insolvency Resolution Process. IB Code was not meant for liquidation of stressed assets but to revive viable assets.

CDR AS A RESOLUTION
MECHANISM FAILED BECAUSE ....

- Restructuring was often done just to delay the classification of an account as NPA rather than making efforts to make it viable
- The interest of banks was in maintaining the account as standard instead of ensuring revival and sustainable operations
- There was no effort on the part of the banks to identify the reasons for sickness and to address them
- The effect of downturn in external environment was often ignored
- Banks were under a wish list syndrome in suggesting models that would be acceptable to their sanctioning authority with an eye on provisioning and NPA management, without considering viability

---

There is a need to make bankers accountable for their action in the process of CIRP. If any company is forced into liquidation due to indecisiveness of bankers or due to their commercially wrong decision, where NPV of resolution is multiple times the liquidation value, then they should be held accountable. Banks need to be questioned for such commercially wrong decisions which go against their interests only because some bankers wish to save themselves from future questioning. It calls for a change in the system.

The bankers should be protected from harassment on commercial decisions of haircut in NCLT driven IB Code while they should also be pulled up for any loss to the banking system and to the productive assets due to their indecision. The Corporate Insolvency Resolution Process can never succeed without active and prudent participation of bankers.

Banks are not expected to close the economy. India is not closing and needs its industries for its people. Washing off its hand from the stressed assets at paltry liquidation value is in effect destruction of assets. Such an approach of banks would result in huge job losses and unemployment would rise multifold. Liquidation of companies at scrap value by the banks, even if the companies are in production, making profit, providing employment to a few thousand people, contributing to the government exchequer by making all tax and statutory payments on time, would be detrimental to the industrial scenario and socio-economic landscape of the country.

We are today at an opportune time to have the industrial development zoom forward because of various initiatives to propel growth taken by the government under the dynamic leadership of Narendra Modi, Prime Minister of India. However, the current approach in CIRP under IB Code 2016 raises serious concern and would certainly be a major damper that can derail the potential growth momentum, causing huge social distress. Government needs to provide proper guidelines and protection to the banks as they tackle the stressed assets.

There is need for an urgent intervention by the government before some valuable companies are condemned to the gallows. This would deal a serious blow to 'Make in India' and 'start up India' killing the entrepreneurial spirit in the country.

Economy: Macro, Micro & More

ADVERT

IB Code - The Euthanasia to kill viable companies?

IB CODE AS THE ICU FOR SICK INDUSTRY HAS KILLED MORE COMPANIES THAN IT COULD REVIVE – EVEN VIABLE COMPANIES WITH OPERATIONAL PLANTS AND LARGE SCALE EMPLOYMENT GET ISSUED DEATH CERTIFICATES LAWYERS AND CONSULTANTS MINTING MONEY WHILE LENDERS AGONISINGLY WAIT FOR CASH

ARUN KUMAR JAGATRAMKA
chairman Gujarat NRE group &
chairman, Assocham National Council on
Ease of Doing Business

The IB Code 2016 is a landmark piece of legislation amongst a horde of path breaking reforms brought in by the current government. This single piece of legislation has allowed us to jump several places in the world ranking, on ease of resolving insolvencies. We at ASSOCHAM applaud this strong and revolutionary reform.

The IB Code addresses most of the important failings of the past, while offering a uniform and comprehensive legislation that allows creditors to assess the viability of a debtor as a business decision, and agree upon a plan for revival.

Then why after 15 months of the IB Code in practice, is the country still failing to tackle NPAs?

> THE LINE BETWEEN A REGULAR BUSINESS CAUGHT IN THE FLUCTUATING GLOBAL AND DOMESTIC ECONOMIC CYCLES, AND A FRAUD, AND/OR A WILLFUL DEFAULTER NEEDS TO BE REDRAWN

Genuine promoter vs willful defaulter and/or fraud

> WE ALREADY HAVE THE MECHANISM TO IDENTIFY FRAUDS, AND WILLFUL DEFAULTERS, SO A BLANKET BAN ON ALL PROMOTERS INCLUDING GENUINE CASES OF DEFAULT DUE TO FACTORS BEYOND HUMAN CONTROL IS PENALISING THE INDIAN ECONOMY AND NEEDS TO BE TWEAKED TO ALLOW GENUINE PROMOTERS TO PARTICIPATE

Early on, just as the IB Code became the go-to tool for banks and industry as hope for revival and recovery, the IB Code Ordinance was introduced in November 2017, quickly becoming an Act preventing promoters from participating in the resolution plan for the revival of their own companies.

This Act had the unintended and unfortunate consequence of painting the genuine promoter and entrepreneur with the same brush as a fraud, and/or a willful defaulter. Equating and further penalising a genuine entrepreneur whose industry has been hit by external factors for reasons beyond their control, and putting them on the stand along with frauds and willful defaulters is akin to punishing an already harassed farmer for drought.

December 2017 saw 40 cases disposed off by the NCLT—30 into liquidation. In other words 75% of businesses hoping, and working for revival were liquidated—banks will never recover the debt of

> IT IS LIKE PENALISING A CANDIDATE FOR LOSING ONE ELECTION BY DEBARRING THEM FOR LIFE FROM CONTESTING ANOTHER ELECTION

75% of the companies in question, the employees of 75% cases joined the ranks of unemployment, 75% of productive assets' have been left to gather rust. In our country a large number of businesses are family-oriented enterprises. The promoter is the life blood of the company and vice-versa. It is rare for a third party to have any interest in that company. By debarring promoters of such companies from trying to revive their own companies, the Act takes away the only chance that these companies have for revival. This means that the company is compulsorily sent for liquidation resulting in loss to the government exchequer, and massive unemployment. In turn this adversely effects the socio-economic fabric of our society.

Personal guarantees—when should they be invoked

> TO INVOKE THE PROMOTERS' PERSONAL GUARANTEE NOW WITHOUT GIVING THEM A CHANCE TO REVIVE THE COMPANY UNDER IB CODE IS THROWING THE BABY WITH THE BATH WATER. IT TREATS THE PROMOTER LIKE A CRIMINAL AND THE INDIAN ENTREPRENEURIAL SPIRIT A CRIME

Every business carries a risk of failure due to various reasons such as recession, competition, etc. Thus historically, entrepreneurs were reluctant to set up new industrial ventures because failure meant recovery. This recovery was done for the loans taken by the business through auction or sale of the businessperson's household and personal effects. To encourage industrialisation and entrepreneurship, the legal principle was created, that if a company is incorporated under the Companies Act, the liability of the shareholders becomes limited. A company was held to be a distinct legal entity separate from its shareholders and directors. This legal principle gave protection to businessmen, and ushered in the era of an industrial revolution.

The new section 29A takes away from the promoter who himself is a victim of the recent severe industrial downturn the chance to revive his embattled company. This is severely detrimental. We would be going back in time when only foreign businesses and big corporates owned the country's resources, while the common Indian citizen remained workers and employees with no say. It is my humble request not to kill entrepreneurship as it would have deep implications on the economy and the society.

Revamping the health of Indian banks

> IN MOST CASES, TANGIBLE VALUE OR LIQUIDATION VALUE OF THE ASSETS MAY NOT BE MUCH, BUT THE EARNING POTENTIAL OF SUCH ASSETS MAY BE MUCH HIGHER WHICH CAN BE CAPTURED ONLY THROUGH THE UPSIDE OF EQUITY VALUE

The current level of NPA includes accrued interest, and interest upon interest while the company was not making profits. Such overdue interest amount whether paid or unpaid, or replaced by corporate loans is seldom backed by security of tangible assets. The asset value itself deteriorates sharply due to bad news.

For the success of any resolution plan, the viable and sustainable debt of the company needs to be worked out, instead of mandating maximum haircut to be allowed.

So for stronger balance sheets, banks need to copy the US model which runs on a mix of debt-equity and instead of ignoring equity, banks should focus on how to maximise their recovery out of equity in cases where banks lost their debt in the past. Holding 60-80% equity as some banks may like to do to maximise their returns will also not help because then the equity value will not be there. For that they need to understand the way equity upside works. Ideally banks should hold around 20-30% in a company, but on a minimum basis they may opt for 40% equity in a company. But in any case, owning above 40% equity in a company will keep the public away from that company and banks will not get any upside. While the public holding should ideally be again a sliver of 30-40%, preferably around 40%, while the rest could be with the promoter to incentivise him to run the company in a professional manner.

> ANY AMOUNT OF RECAPITALISATION WILL NOT HELP UNLESS THE BANKS STRENGTHEN THEIR SYSTEMS AND TRY TO RECOVER AS MUCH AS POSSIBLE FROM THE NPAS INSTEAD OF CONSIGNING THE COMPANIES TO THE FLAMES IN TOTO. RECENTLY, THE BANKS ARE RELUCTANT TO ACCEPT ANY PROPOSAL WHERE THEY NEED TO TAKE LARGE HAIRCUTS. INSTEAD STRANGELY, THEY CHOOSE LIQUIDATION IGNORING RECOVERY HOWEVER SMALL. THE ADDITIONAL POTENTIAL OF EQUITY UPSIDE IS TOTALLY IGNORED. THE EFFECT OF THIS LIQUIDATION ON OTHER STAKEHOLDERS LIKE EMPLOYEES, SUPPLIERS, CUSTOMERS AND PUBLIC SHAREHOLDERS IS TOTALLY IGNORED. THIS APPROACH NEEDS TO BE QUESTIONED, AND COMMERCIALLY OPTIMISED DECISIONS NEED TO BE TAKEN BY THE BANKS IN THE INTEREST OF ALL STAKEHOLDERS

The Economic Times—15 March 2018

IB CODE-THE EUTHANASIA TO KILL VIABLE COMPANIES?

Ib code as the ICU for sick industry has killed more companies than it could revive—even viable companies with operational plants and large scale employment get issued death certificates—lawyers and consultants minting money while lenders agonisingly wait for cash

The IB Code 2016 is a landmark piece of legislation amongst a horde of path breaking reforms brought in by the current government. This single piece of legislation has allowed us to jump several places in the world ranking on ease of resolving insolvencies. We at ASSOCHAM applaud this strong and revolutionary reform.

The IB Code addresses most of the important failings of the past, while offering a uniform and comprehensive legislation that allows creditors to assess the viability of a debtor as a business decision, and agree upon a plan for revival.

Then why after 15 months of the IB Code in practice, is the country still failing to tackle NPAs?

THE LINE BETWEEN A REGULAR BUSINESS CAUGHT IN THE FLUCTUATING GLOBAL AND DOMESTIC ECONOMIC CYCLES, AND A FRAUD, AND/OR A WILLFUL DEFAULTER NEEDS TO BE REDRAWN

Genuine promoter vs willful defaulter and/or fraud

WE ALREADY HAVE THE MECHANISM TO IDENTIFY FRAUDS, AND WILLFUL DEFAULTERS, SO A BLANKET BAN ON ALL PROMOTERS INCLUDING GENUINE CASES OF DEFAULT DUE TO FACTORS BEYOND HUMAN CONTROL IS PENALISING THE INDIAN ECONOMY AND NEED TO BE TWEAKED TO ALLOW GENUINE PROMOTERS TO PARTICIPATE

Early on, just as the IB Code became the go-to tool for banks and industry as hope for revival and recovery, the IB Code Ordinance was introduced in November 2017, quickly becoming an Act preventing promoters from participating in the resolution plan for the revival of their own companies.

This Act had the unintended and unfortunate consequence of painting the genuine promoter and entrepreneur with the same brush as a fraud, and/ or a willful defaulter. Equating and further penalizing a genuine entrepreneur whose industry has been hit by external factors for reasons beyond their control, and putting them on the stand along with frauds and willful defaulters is akin to punishing an already harassed farmer for drought.

December 2017 saw 40 cases disposed off [*sic*] by the NCLT—30 into liquidation. In other words 75 per cent of businesses hoping, and working for revival were liquidated—banks will never recover the debt of 75 per cent of the companies in question, the employees of 75 per cent cases joined the ranks of unemployment, 75 per cent of productive assets have been left to gather rust. In our country a large number of businesses are family-promoted enterprises. The promoter is the life blood of the company and vice-versa. It is rare for a third party to have any interest in that company. By debarring promoters of such companies from trying to revive their own companies, the Act takes away the only chance that these companies have for revival. This means that the company is compulsorily sent for liquidation resulting in loss to the government exchequer, and massive unemployment. In turn this adversely affects the socio-economic fabric of our society.

Personal guarantees—when should they be invoked

TO INVOKE THE PROMOTERS' PERSONAL GUARANTEE NOW WITHOUT GIVING THEM A CHANCE TO REVIVE THE COMPANY UNDER IB CODE IS THROWING THE BABY WITH THE BATH WATER. IT MAKES THE PROMOTER A CRIMINAL AND THE INDIAN ENTREPRENEURIAL SPIRIT A CRIME

Every business carries a risk of failure due to various reasons such as recession, competition, etc. Thus historically, entrepreneurs were reluctant to set up new industrial ventures because failure meant recovery. This recovery was done for the loans taken by the business through auction or sale of the businessperson's household and personal effects. To encourage industrialisation and entrepreneurship, the legal principle was created, that if a company is incorporated under the Companies Act, the liability of the shareholders becomes limited. A company was held to be a distinct legal entity separate from its shareholders and directors. This legal principle gave protection to businessmen and ushered in the era of an industrial revolution.

The new section 29A takes away from the promoter who himself is a victim of the recent severe industrial downturn the chance to revive his embattled company. This is severely detrimental. We would be going back in time when only foreign businesses and big corporates owned the country's resources, while the common Indian citizen remained workers and employees with no say. It is my humble request not to kill entrepreneurship as it would have deep implications on the economy and the society.

Revamping the health of Indian banks

IN MOST CASES, TANGIBLE VALUE OR LIQUIDATION VALUE OF THE ASSETS MAY NOT BE MUCH, BUT THE EARNING POTENTIAL OF SUCH ASSETS MAY BE MUCH HIGHER WHICH CAN BE CAPTURED ONLY THROUGH THE UPSIDE OF EQUITY VALUE

The current level of NPA includes accrued interest, and interest upon interest while the company was not making profits. Such overdue interest amount whether paid or unpaid, or replaced by corporate loans is seldom backed by security of tangible assets. The asset value itself deteriorates sharply due to bad news.

For the success of any resolution plan, the viable and sustainable debt of the company needs to be worked out, instead of mandating maximum haircut to be allowed.

So for stronger balance sheets, banks need to copy the LIC model which runs on a mix of debt-equity and instead of ignoring equity, banks should focus on how to maximise their recovery out of equity in cases where banks lost their debt in the past. Holding 80-90 per cent equity as some banks may like to do to maximise their returns will also not help because then the equity value will not be there. For that they need to understand the way equity upside works. Ideally banks should hold around 20-30 per cent in a company, but on a maximum basis they may opt for 40 per cent equity in a company. But in any case, owning above 40 per cent equity in a company will keep the public away from that company and banks will not get any upside. While the public holding should ideally be again a similar of 30-40 per cent, preferably around 40 per cent, while the rest could be with the promoter to incentivise him to run the company in a professional manner.

ANY AMOUNT OF RECAPITALISATION WILL NOT HELP UNLESS THE BANKS STRENGTHEN THEIR SYSTEMS AND TRY TO RECOVER AS MUCH AS POSSIBLE FROM THE NPAS INSTEAD OF CONSIGNING THE COMPANIES TO THE FLAMES IN TOTO. RECENTLY, THE BANKS ARE RELUCTANT TO ACCEPT ANY PROPOSAL WHERE THEY NEED TO TAKE LARGE HAIRCUTS. INSTEAD STRANGELY, THEY CHOOSE LIQUIDATION IGNORING RECOVERY HOWEVER SMALL. THE ADDITIONAL POTENTIAL OF EQUITY UPSIDE IS TOTALLY IGNORED. THE EFFECT OF THIS LIQUIDATION ON OTHER STAKEHOLDERS LIKE EMPLOYEES, SUPPLIERS, CUSTOMERS AND PUBLIC SHAREHOLDERS IS TOTALLY IGNORED. THIS APPROACH NEEDS TO BE QUESTIONED, AND COMMERCIALLY OPTIMISED DECISIONS NEED TO BE TAKEN BY THE BANKS IN THE INTEREST OF ALL STAKEHOLDERS.

Business Standard   THURSDAY, 6 JUNE 2019

DOES INDIAN INDUSTRY HAVE A PLACE IN MODI'S "NEW INDIA"?

Congratulations india! We have succeeded in finally demolishing the layers of divisive politics that have plagued us, and forced us into bad choices, leading to—wide-scale poverty, inadequate infrastructure, measly reforms, horrendous corruption, empty political gestures and slogans, and unacceptable dynasties within our robust democracy.

The actual implementation of the many schemes and reforms on the ground— irrespective of the vote shares – by the Modi-led government in the past five years has translated into this confidence in our democracy.

Instead of the poor, the incumbent government has actually attempted to tackle poverty and other problems through sustainable schemes with long-term goals. Similarly, **Indian industry too is in dire need of much sought-after reforms.**

Having been slaves for centuries, Indians have been habitual rule breakers and protesters and could never consider themselves as part of the establishment mainly due to the step-motherly treatment that continued to be meted out by the people in power even after independence who continued with the British legacy.

With digitisation, introduction of GST and Modi Govt's stress on clean governance, most of such **innocent law breakers who were forced to evade the law till now could henceforth do business in a clean and transparent manner.** But in the absence of any transitional provision and unlimited powers in the hands of enforcement agencies found themselves caught in the whirlpool of never-ending investigations.

A simple limitation period of, say, anywhere from 3 to 5 years for initiating any investigation under any law by any enforcement agency would have allowed most of such past forced offenders to become fully compliant honest citizens of India instead of constantly living under fear and perpetuating the wrongs done by them earlier.

The current environment of witch hunting in the country where every industrialist is treated a bigger criminal as compared to dacoity and murder and the entire nation is found baying for his blood has done some serious harm in the eco system **where a large part of the educated upper middle class has decided to migrate out of the country.** While the individual may be penalized and/or blacklisted,

there is no reason to do so to all his children & grandchildren who are otherwise marked for life having been born in the wrong family.

As against our dream of a free India where every citizen could hold his head high, we find ourselves today under a constant fear of Enforcement agency officials who can pick any individual or group of individuals at their whims and harass and torture without assigning any reason and without any accountability.

All they need is to frame some flimsy charges against the individual and rest of the needful is done by masala story hungry 24 hour news channels to hang the individual even before he could understand the charges slapped on him. **Somebody very rightly said that in India we don't have RULE OF LAW but RULE OF MEN.**

The Bankruptcy Law Reforms Committee (BLRC) envisioned the IBC as "a collective mechanism for resolving insolvency within a framework of equity and fairness to all stakeholders to preserve economic value in the process". However, due to arbitrary & indiscriminate amendments **IBC is neither fair nor equitable to all stakeholders and due to never ending litigations has also failed to** preserve economic value.

The IB Code was designed to be more inclusive in approach and there was definitely no intention to avoid promoters from submitting resolution plans. However, the effect of Section 29A is exactly opposite to the preamble to the IB Code as set by the BLRC.

This also had the unintended, and unfortunate consequence of painting the genuine promoter and entrepreneur with the same brush as a fraud, and/or a wilful defaulter. **The line between a regular business caught in the fluctuating global and domestic economic cycles, and a fraud, and/or a willful defaulter needs to be redrawn.**

Most affected in the current environment is the vast rural population who are looking at large scale job losses due to continued industrial slowdown as well as forced liquidation of even otherwise viable and operating companies due to inconsistencies in the newly introduced IB Code.

However, to ensure that the defaulting promoters who could not save their company from external downturn, do not get back their Companies for a song, a premium of say, 20% could be applied over the highest 3rd party bid for comparison with the promoters' bid. This would ensure that the promoters pay

Arun Kumar Jagatramka
Chairman, Centre for Growth and Sustainable Development, FMSDGs & Group Chairman, Gujarat NRE

substantially higher amount than anybody else is willing to pay and would also lead to much higher recovery for the lenders. This would also reduce litigation in a large number of cases and lead to much faster and quicker resolution as compared to the present scenario of long drawn uncertainty.

In the current environment, public shareholders, particularly small investors are the silent sufferers since any new resolution applicant destroys existing equity value in toto while the shareholders lose everything even otherwise if the company is liquidated. The interest of public shareholders can be safeguarded in a much better manner if the existing promoters is allowed to revive the company where all stakeholders participate in future upside from operations.

Limited liability to unlimited sorrow: Concept of limited liability was the lifeblood of industrial development in 20th century and any proposal to change the law in a manner

that would punish the promoter for business failure which are at times beyond his control for various external factors is against the principle of natural justice. It would kill the entrepreneurship in the country as people would shy away from setting an industry. The most affected would be the individual entrepreneur, where the promoters are forced to provide personal guarantee and this move would kill such business and discourage new entrepreneurs to take the risk.

We would be going back in time where foreign businesses and big corporates will be owning everything making entire country slaves or employees for themselves.

There is need for an urgent intervention by the government before the Indian entrepreneurial spirit meets an untimely death and invaded by foreign powers.

ADVERTORIAL

The Foundation for Millennium Sustainable Development Goals (MSDGs)
www.foundationformsdgs.com • E-mail: connect@foundationformsdgs.com

Business Standard—6 June 2019

DOES INDIAN INDUSTRY HAVE A PLACE IN MODI'S "NEW INDIA"?

Congratulations India! We have succeeded in finally demolishing the layers of divisive politics that have plagued us, and forced us into bad choices, leading to—widescale poverty, inadequate infrastructure, measly reforms, horrendous corruption, empty political gestures and slogans, and unacceptable dynasties within our robust democracy.

The actual implementation of the many schemes and reforms on the ground—irrespective of the vote shares—by the Modi-led government in the past five years has translated into this confidence in our democracy.

Instead of the poor, the incumbent government has actually attempted to tackle poverty and other problems through sustainable schemes with long-term goals. **Similarly, Indian industry too is in direct need of such sought-after reforms**.

Having been slaves for centuries, Indians have been habitual rule breakers and protesters and could never consider themselves as part of the establishment mainly due to the step-motherly treatment that continued to be meted out by the people in power even after independence who continued with the British legacy.

With digitisation, introduction of GST and Modi Govt's stress on clean governance, most of such **innocent law breakers who were forced to evade the law till now could henceforth do business in a clean and transparent manner**. But in the absence of any transitional provision and unlimited powers in the hands of enforcement agencies found themselves caught in the whirlpool of never-ending investigations.

A simple limitation period of, say, anywhere from 3 to 5 years for initiating any investigation under any law by any enforcement agency could have allowed most of such past forced offenders to become fully compliant honest citizens of India instead of constantly living under fear and perpetuating the wrongs done by them earlier.

The current environment of witch hunting in the country where every industrialist is treated a bigger criminal as compared to dacoity and murder and the entire nation is found baying for his blood has done some serious harm in the eco-system **where a large part of the educated upper middle**

class has decided to migrate out of the country. While the individual may be penalized and/or blacklisted, there is no reason to do so to all his children & grandchildren who are otherwise marked for life having been born in the wrong family.

As against our dream of a free India where every citizen could hold his head high, we find ourselves today under a constant fear of Enforcement agency officials who can pick any individual or group of individuals at their whims and harass and torture without assigning any reason and without any accountability.

All they need is to frame some flimsy charges against the individual and rest of the needful is done by masala story hungry 24 hour news channels to hang the individual even before he could understand the charges slapped on him. **Somebody very rightly said that in India we don't have RULE OF LAW but RULE OF MEN.**

The Bankruptcy Law Reforms Committee (BLRC) envisioned the IBC as "a collective mechanism for resolving insolvency within a framework of equity and fairness to all stakeholders to preserve economic value in the process". However, due to arbitrary & indiscriminate amendments **IBC is neither fair nor equitable to all stakeholders and due to never ending litigations has also failed to preserve economic value.**

The IB Code was designated to be more inclusive in approach and there was definitely no intention to avoid promoters from submitting resolution plans. However, the effect of Section 29A is exactly opposite to the preamble to the IB Code as set by the BLRC.

This also had the unintended, and unfortunate consequence of painting the genuine promoter and entrepreneur with the same brush as a fraud, and/ or a wilful defaulter. **The line between a regular business caught in the fluctuating global and domestic economic cycles, and a fraud, and/or a wilful defaulter needs to be redrawn.**

Most affected in the current environment is the vast rural population who are looking at large scale job losses due to continued industrial slowdown as well as forced liquidation of even otherwise viable and operating companies due to inconsistencies in the newly introduced IB Code.

However, to ensure that the defaulting promoters who could not save their company from external downturn, do not get back their Companies for a song, a premium of say, 20 per cent could be applied over the highest

3rd party bid for comparison with the promoters' bid. This would ensure that the promoters pay substantially higher amount than anybody else is willing to pay and would also lead to much faster and quicker resolution as compared to the present scenario of long drawn uncertainty.

In the current environment, public shareholders, particularly small investors are the silent sufferers since any new resolution applicant destroys existing equity value in toto while the shareholders lose everything even otherwise if the company is liquidated. The interest of public shareholders can be safeguarded in a much better manner if the existing promoters is allowed to revive the company where all stakeholders participate in future upside from operations.

Limited liability to unlimited sorrow: Concept of limited liability was the lifeblood of industrial development in 20th century and any proposal to change the law in a manner that would punish the promoter for business failure which are at times beyond his control for various external factors is against the principle of natural justice. It would kill the entrepreneurship in the country as people would shy away from setting an industry. The most affected would be the individual entrepreneur, where the promoters are forced to provide personal guarantee and this move would kill such business and discourage new entrepreneurs to take the risk.

WHILE THE GOVERNMENT IS FOCUSSED ON A SUSTAINED GROWTH OF OUR ECONOMY, THE INDIAN INDUSTRY WHICH CONTRIBUTES TO 26 per cent OF THE COUNTRY's GDP SEEMS TO HAVE BEEN LEFT ON THE WAYSIDE, UNPROTECTED, AND MARKED FOR CRIMINALIZATION. WHY?

We would be going back in time where foreign businesses and big corporates will be owning everything making entire country slaves or employees for themselves.

There is need for an urgent intervention by the government before the Indian entrepreneurial spirit meets an untimely death and invaded by foreign powers.

Business Standard KOLKATA | MONDAY, 1 JULY 2019 **5**

Modi Opens 2nd Innings Hitting Corruption for a Six

Celebrating 2 Anniversary of GST

In a new drive for "Swachh Bharat", the government has compulsorily retired 27 senior officers of the central tax administration who were facing charges of corruption and illegal gratification. To start with, this is certainly a very welcome step and the nation remains hungry for much more.

However, instead of punishing the corrupt, a Golden Handshake with 3 months pay thrown in to enjoy the rest of their lives with the loot could not be appreciated. Unless the corrupt get actual convictions and finality with all appeals exhausted in a swift timely fashion, things cannot change.

For too long we have had the *Chalta Hai* attitude and the honest few have been at the receiving end. It's time to reverse the trend and instill fear of law in the corrupt by certainty of punishment in a fast track mode.

Antiquated and complicated non compliable laws have fueled unbridled corruption leading to a mindset where corruption is perceived as their birthright. This perception needs to be changed for things to improve. Excessive criminalization of all commercial laws has led to the entire population under duress to submit to all sorts of illegitimate demands whether guilty or not.

GST in addition to usual teething trouble contains a few minor irritants which seems to have been thrown in to feed the invisible elephant of corruption.

A close inspection of the tax laws and structure in India reveals quite a few disturbing facts. There are serious ambiguities in GST on transportation, overlap in customs duty & GST on ocean freight, barges, coastal movement of cargo and valuation in volatile markets.

For example, GST on head office rendering services to plant and branches within the same company, reverse charge mechanism, GST on advance payments, GST on unpaid invoices, separate registration in each state negating ONE NATION ONE TAX totally, anamoly in multiple jurisdictions of central and state – a major tool for harassment, loss of input credit to buyer for default by supplier, etc.

Most of these issues have negligible revenue impact but remain a major tool for harassment and corruption. In addition unlimited power to reopen past assessments and endless scrutiny until settled through corruption remain a major pain point for all businesses specially MSMEs.

The Indian tax laws are a legacy of the socialist era that was an adversarial system tilted towards enforcement rather than compliance. India also has the history of high rate of corporate tax – even the current 30-40% tax is higher than that in competitor nations. Sadly, instead of reducing tax to incentivize private sector, policy makers have tried to bypass the system with a maze of deductions and exemptions. Fear among successive governments of not being branded as pro-business has always been at work. This is the reason for which tax terrorism flourished in India.

Sadly, one black sheep in the industry forces others to evade giving rise to the sibling effect. There is an urgent need to single out the black sheep and not paint the entire industry with the same brush.

The cumbersome filing of long and complicated tax forms is a tax payer's nightmare. Simplification would increase tax net. Small shop keeper, businessmen may want to pay tax but cannot afford time or money to fill the tax forms. For them, bribing the tax inspector remains a much easier option.

Tax Raids have no place in a civilized society, but they continue because officials enjoy the power that allows them to humiliate the rich and famous, and also allow them to make extra money.

Raids, search and seizures only vitiate the industrial climate and leads to trust deficit on both sides. In today's digital era information can be obtained by the click of a button, hence such measures are obsolete; they are reminiscent of the feudal legacy and need to be done away with except in rarest of the rare cases.

The government must initiate actions which make it clear that the Indian taxman is equipped with the necessary knowledge of when to use the law and not a 'Tax Terrorist' who indiscriminately uses the tax laws to cause discontent.

For several centuries, Indians being slaves were brainwashed to distrust other Indians. Distrust saps national energy, kills initiative and compels manipulation. Trust and transparency promotes entrepreneurship. We must learn to trust each other.

Arun Kumar Jagatramka
Chairman, Centre for Growth and Sustainable Development, FMSDGs & Group Chairman, Gujarat NRE

We should be in a system in which people are honest because they want to be, not because they have to be. The law-makers and government machineries must understand that trust based system provides great advantages, promotes entrepreneurship, and not by seeking revenge to stop doing business.

Indian industry has been struggling for last few years and urgently needs hand-holding by the Government to come out of the current crisis mode and positively contribute to nation building.

For a corruption-free and fully compliant society, we need to get on the right track and that too on an immediate basis:

- Decriminalise the commercial laws
- Remove minor irritants in tax laws which have negligible revenue impact but very high corruption impact and are a major source of heartburn
- Reduce litigation and the overload on judicial system by doing away with routine appeals by Govt. in all matters
- Initiate regular interaction between very senior level tax officials from Delhi & people across the country twice a year aimed at reducing the ground level corruption
- Ensure timely closure of all investigations - prescribed timelines for investigations and closure of cases
- Strict 3 year limitation for initiation and maximum one year for judgments
- If anyone is found not guilty, he/she should be notified accordingly
- Ongoing electronic surveillance and 360 degree profiling to ensure voluntary compliance
- Certainty of punishment based on such surveillance & profiling

The Foundation for Millennium Sustainable Development Goals (MSDGs)
Contact: Ph. 011-41767807 • Deept (M) 9717936640 • www.foundationformsdgs.com, E-mail: connect@foundationformsdgs.com

ADVERTORIAL

Business Standard—1 July 2019

MODI OPENS 2ND INNINGS HITTING CORRUPTION FOR A SIX
Celebrating 2nd Anniversary of GST

In a new drive for "Swachh Bharat", the government has compulsorily retired 27 senior officers of the central tax administration who were facing charges of corruption and illegal gratification. To start with, this is certainly a very welcome step and the nation remains hungry for much more.

However, instead of punishing the corrupt, a Golden Handshake with 3 months pay thrown in to enjoy the rest of their lives with the loot could not be appreciated. Unless the corrupt get actual convictions and finality with all appeals exhausted in a swift timely fashion, things cannot change.

For too long we have had the *Chalta Hai* attitude and the honest few have been at the receiving end. It's time to reverse the trend and instill fear of law in the corrupt by certainty of punishment in a fast track mode.

Antiquated and complicated non compliable laws have fueled unbridled corruption leading to a mindset where corruption is perceived as their birthright. This perception needs to be changed for things to improve. Excessive criminalization of all commercial laws has led to the entire population under duress to submit to all sorts of illegitimate demands whether guilty or not.

GST in addition to usual teething trouble contains a few minor irritants which seems to have been thrown in to feed the invisible elephant of corruption

A close inspection of the tax laws and structure in India reveals quite a few disturbing facts. There are serious ambiguities in GST on transportation, overlap in customs duty & GST on ocean freight, barges, coastal movement of cargo and valuation in volatile markets.

For example, GST on head office rendering services to plant and branches within the same company, reverse charge mechanism, GST on advance payments, GST on unpaid invoices, separate registration in each state negating ONE NATION ONE TAX totally, anamoly in multiple jurisdiction of central and state—a major tool for harassment, loss of input credit to buyer for default by supplier, etc.

Most of these issues have negligible revenue impact but remain a major tool for harassment and corruption. In addition unlimited power to reopen past assessments and endless scrutiny until settled through corruption remain a major pain point for all businesses specially MSMEs.

The Indian tax laws are a legacy of the socialist era that was an adversarial system tilted towards enforcement rather than compliance. India also has the history of high rate of corporate tax—even the current 30-40 per cent tax is higher than that in competitor nations. Sadly, instead of reducing tax to incentivize private sector, policy makers have tried to bypass the system with a maze of deductions and exemptions. Fear among successive governments of not being branded as pro-business has always been at work. This is the reason for which tax terrorism flourished in India.

Sadly, one black sheep in the industry forces others to evade giving rise to the sibling effect. There is an urgent need to single out the black sheep and not paint the entire industry with the same brush.

The cumbersome filing of long and complicated tax forms is a tax payer's nightmare. Simplification would increase tax net. Small shop keeper, businessmen may want to pay tax but cannot afford time or money to fill the tax forms. For them, bribing the tax inspector remains a much easier option.

Tax Raids have no place in a civilized society, but they continue because officials enjoy the power that allows them to humiliate the rich and famous, and also allow them to make extra money.

Raids, search and seizures only vitiate the industrial climate and leads to trust deficit on both sides. In today's digital era information can be obtained by the click of a button, hence such measures are obsolete; they are reminiscent of the feudal legacy and need to be done away with except in rarest of the rare cases.

The government must initiate actions which make it clear that the Indian taxman is equipped with the necessary knowledge of when to use the law and not a 'Tax Terrorist' who indiscriminately uses the tax laws to cause discontent.

We should be in a system in which people are honest because they want to be, not because they have to be. The law-makers and government machineries must understand that trust based system provides great advantages, promotes entrepreneurship, and not by seeking revenge to stop doing business.

Indian Industry has been struggling for last few years and urgently needs hand-holding by the Government to come out of the current crisis mode and positively contribute to nation building.

For a corruption free fully compliant society, we need to get on the right track and that too on an immediate basis:

- Decriminalise commercial laws
- Remove minor irritants in tax laws which have negligible revenue impact but very high corruption impact and a major source of heartburn
- Reduce litigation and the overload on judicial system by doing away with routine appeal by Govt. in all matters
- Initiate regular interaction between Very Senior level tax officials from Delhi and people across the country twice a year aimed at reducing the ground level corruption
- Ensure Timely closure of all investigations - prescribed timelines for investigation and closure of cases
- Strict 3 year limitation for initiation and maximum one year for judgments
- If anyone is found not guilty, he should be notified accordingly
- Certainty of punishment

For several centuries, Indians being slaves were brainwashed to distrust other Indians. Distrust saps national energy, kills initiative and compels manipulation. Trust and transparency promotes entrepreneurship. We must learn to trust each other.

usiness Standard KOLKATA | FRIDAY, 26 JULY 2019

India needs Court Transcripts to tackle Corruption in Judiciary

How do we hold a judge accountable? How do we ensure that the judgement pronounced matches with the arguments at the hearing? How do we try and close one door of corruption in our justice system?

The answer: Court Transcripts

The judicial courts of India have always found it hard to shrug off the label of corruption in their corridors. Recently this stench of corruption even reached the inner chambers of the judges of the Supreme Court where orders were found to be rewritten by court masters for the benefit of one party as against what was originally ordered by the judge in open court.

It was caught by an eagle-eyed lawyer and brought to the attention of the judges. Luckily the judges remembered their original decision and saw the discrepancy and the order could be corrected. But does it not then make you wonder how many orders are incorrectly written and different from what the judges say?

Ideally you would expect the judges and the lawyers to remember. But the Indian judiciary is massively overburdened with the dates between hearings so long that it could be months or sometimes even years. The famous Sunny Deol line, *"Tareekh pe Tareekh, Tareekh pe Tareekh..."* is not only a famous dialogue now but a sad reality of the justice system in India.

Insiders would vouch that there are ample examples of judgements delivered months after the hearings being dramatically opposed to the arguments made and accepted by the judges at the hearing. In the absence of any check or mechanism on such anomalies the only remedy is the appellate forum. But the problem gets compounded if the judgements in appeal are equally vitiated in the absence of any official record of what actually transpired at the appeals' hearing.

That's why, we still don't have RULE OF LAW but what we have could be loosely labeled as RULE OF MEN.

How do we hold a judge accountable? How do we ensure that the judgement pronounced matches with the arguments at the hearing? How do we try and close one door of corruption in our justice system?

The answer: Court Transcripts

Perhaps many in India would have heard the words, Court Transcript for the first time. But it is an embedded part of the judicial system for all western and developed countries like Australia, UK and USA, to name a few.

It is also not a very complicated and expensive procedure and can be added to our Indian courts easily. Basically the proceedings of the court are voice recorded and simultaneously typed on the day itself by stenographers.

The transcript becomes an exact record of every word spoken by any such person as indicated which includes the judges, barristers, lawyers and witnesses etc.

The transcript can also be helpful to refresh one's memory in our judicial system where the dates between hearings are so long that the judges roster itself changes before

Arun Kumar Jagatramka
Chairman, Centre for Growth and
Sustainable Development, FMSDGs
& Group Chairman, Gujarat NRE

a matter comes up again. It can help the parties and the judges to see what arguments have been taken and where the hearing concluded with what remarks, so that repetition may be avoided and time may be saved for future.

Simply put, a transcript makes those in open court be accountable for their words. Judges can be shown what was said in the last hearing. It can also ensure that a clean and respectable hearing takes place without the unnecessary mudslinging that has become so prevalent in India.

At the very end it will ensure that a poorer party does not get screwed over by a richer party with deeper pockets willing to spend it in unlawful ways and true justice can be upheld.

Many great minds and eminent personalities including Chief Justices, Judges of the Supreme Court, the High Courts, the Law Ministers, the Law Commission, media, etc. have all lamented over the delay in the dispensation of justice in India, but little to nothing has been done to ensure the swift delivery of justice and that too without corruption.

FMSDGs: Committed to Sustainable Development

With poverty alleviation being one of the most important goals for Foundation for Millennium Sustainable Development Goals, it is difficult to envisage achieving them till the menace of corruption is eradicated from all levels. To do so, it is imperative to bring governments, businesses, civil society organisations and individuals on board to stimulate actions for humane progress.

The Foundation for Millennium Sustainable Development Goals (FMSDGs)
Contact: Ph. 011-41787887 • Deepti (M) 9717838540 • www.foundationformsdgs.com, E-mail: connect@foundationformsdgs.com

ADVERTORIAL

Business Standard—26 July 2019

INDIA NEEDS COURT TRANSCRIPTS TO TACKLE CORRUPTION IN JUDICIARY

HOW DO WE HOLD A JUDGE ACCOUNTABLE? HOW DO WE ENSURE THAT THE JUDGEMENT PRONOUNCED MATCHES WITH THE ARGUMENTS AT THE HEARING? HOW DO WE TRY AND CLOSE ONE DOOR OF CORRUPTION IN OUR JUSTICE SYSTEM?

THE ANSWER : COURT TRANSCRIPTS

The judicial courts of India have always found it hard to shrug off the label of corruption in their corridors. Recently this stench of corruption even reached the inner chambers of the judges of the Supreme Court where orders were found to be rewritten by court masters for the benefit of one party as against what was originally ordered by the judge in open court.

It was caught by an eagle eyed lawyer and brought to the attention of the judges. Luckily the judges remembered their original decision and saw the discrepancy and the order could be corrected. But does it not then make you wonder how many orders are incorrectly written and different from what the judges say?

Ideally you would expect the judges and the lawyers to remember. But the Indian judiciary is massively overburdened with the dates between hearings so long that it could be months or sometimes even years. The famous Sunny Deol line, *"Tareekh pe Tareekh pe Tareekh...."* is not only a famous dialogue now but a sad reality of the justice system in India.

Insiders would vouch that there are ample examples of judgements delivered months after the hearings being dramatically opposed to the arguments made and accepted by the judges at the hearing. In the absence of any check or mechanism on such anomalies the only remedy is the appellate forum. But the problem gets compounded if the judgements in appeal are equally vitiated in the absence of any official record of what actually transpired at the appeals' hearing.

That's why, we still don't have RULE OF LAW but what we have could be loosely labelled as RULE OF MEN.

How do we hold a judge accountable? How do we ensure that the judgement pronounced matches with the arguments at the hearings? How do we try and close one door of corruption in our justice system?

The answer: Court Transcripts

Perhaps many in India would have heard the words, Court Transcript for the first time. But it is an embedded part of the judicial system for all western and developed countries like Australia, UK and USA, to name a few.

It is also not a very complicated and expensive procedure and can be added to our Indian courts easily. Basically the proceedings of the court are voice recorded and simultaneously typed on the day itself by stenographers.

The transcript becomes an exact record of every word spoken by any such person as indicated which includes the judges, barristers, lawyers and witnesses etc.

The transcript can also be helpful to refresh one's memory in our judicial system where the dates between hearings are so long that the judges roster itself changes before a matter comes up again. It can help the parties and the judges to see what arguments have been taken and where the hearing concluded with what remarks, so that repetition may be avoided and time may be saved for future.

Simply put, a transcript makes those in open court be accountable for their words. Judges can be shown what was said in the last hearing. It can also ensure that a clean and respectable hearing takes place without the unnecessary mudslinging that has become so prevalent in India.

At the very end it will ensure that a poorer party does not get screwed over by a richer party with deeper pockets willing to spend it in unlawful ways and true justice can be upheld.

Many great minds and eminent personalities including Chief Justices, Judges of the Supreme Court, the High Courts, the Law Ministers, the Law Commission, media, etc. have all lamented over the delay in the dispensation of justice in India, but little to nothing has been done to ensure the swift delivery of justice and that too without corruption.

Business Standard   KOLKATA | WEDNESDAY, 14 AUGUST 2019

We are Indians and We are NOT CHORS!

72 years is a long time to break the shackles of slavery –
On our 73rd Independence day, let all Indians be truly free.

Say it with me-

I AM AN INDIAN, AND I AM NOT A CRIMINAL.

Arun Kumar Jagatramka
Chairman, Centre for Growth and Sustainable Development,
FMSDGs & Group Chairman, Gujarat NRE

For millennia, India has been the **"Golden Bird"**—सोने की चिड़िया—much looted, ravaged, lorded over, caged, and colonized by a plethora of consecutive non-Indians, who took advantage of our own petty differences that divide us from within.

Obviously, these non-Indians were more interested in their private wealth-collection, rather than the development and wealth-creation of India and Indians. A great example of this is **Robert Clive's**—the person who established the military and political supremacy of the East India Company in India—**infamous defence for the corruption charges brought against him in the British parliament**—

"... an opulent city lay at my mercy; its richest bankers bid against each other for my smiles; I walked through vaults which were thrown open to me alone, piled on either hand with gold and jewels! By God, Mr. Chairman, at this moment I stand astonished at my own moderation."

Consequently, the systems and the laws that they created—which we have inherited are—

- blindingly opaque
- designed to amplify the farcical differences that we Indians believe differentiate us
- while putting unimaginably monopolistic and discriminatory powers in the hands of a few

On 15th August, 1947 when our parents, grandparents, and great-grandparents finally—finally took back control over our own destinies, the men and women who drafted the Constitution of India understood the enormous responsibility that they had undertaken, and so, rightly they called our democracy—**The Great Indian Experiment.**

But a lie repeated enough times begins to start sounding like the truth. For millennia, **Indians have been called thieves and criminals by those actually looting us**—so much so that we have sadly begun to believe it ourselves.

72 years is a long time to break the shackles of slavery – On our 73rd Independence day, let all Indians be truly free. Say it with me—

I AM AN INDIAN, AND I AM NOT A CRIMINAL.

Today, we have the means, the will, and the technology to make our laws, and our systems TRANSPARENT.

Let us further The Great Indian Experiment. For example let's take the Income Tax Department. How can we make it more robust, and free of corruption—

- **Abolish TAX TARGETS.** Incomes fluctuate from year to year.
  - Use data analysis, and data management to determine what the tax for a given period of time for every entity should be.
- Reform the duties of the **tax officers** to **become tax-processors**, instead of the present "tax-collectors".
- The onus needs to rest with the tax-officer to prove, and justify the need to even communicate with a taxpayer, let alone raid an Indian citizen's dignity without notice.
- **Harness the technology of Blockchain**
  - Each taxpayer using his/her unique key will be able to see the breakdown of where our tax rupees is being utilised—police, education, infrastructure, transport, health, arts, research, etc.
  - Because of the immutability of blockchain, any leakages enroute will be immediately identified, and addressed. Thus ensuring Certainty of Punishment.
  - When we Indians begin to see, and experience the benefits of our hard-earned rupees actually being utilised in public facilities that make our day-to-day lives easier, safer, and more convenient—taxes will be filed honestly, and regularly.

We already have a capable, and skilled Finance Minister, who for the first time in our democratic history began her maiden budget speech by honouring honest tax-payers—you and me. Who understands, and does not shy away from addressing the lacunae in our system.

The Modi government is actively on a **"Swachch Bharat Mission"**, taking concrete steps to deter corruption at all stages. But a nation dreaming, and endeavouring to become a $5 trillion dollar economy, cannot afford to treat and harass its citizens like common criminals.

It needs to provide the citizens a period of transition.

When the previously established system promoted corruption, and compelled citizens to navigate daily life only by paying bribes, and untoward favours to the few with monopolistic powers—the new system endeavouring to create a transparent and non-corrupt environment needs to give the citizens the time, and the confidence to live a life free of corruption.

We must understand, if there is an Indian offering and/or putting currency notes under the table, there is another Indian sitting opposite demanding and/or receiving those notes under the table too. Villifying just one party is extremely unfair, and betrays our prejudices.

A few steps that we can take to redesign our system to be transparent and corruption-free are—

- **Put a strict 3 year limitation on initiating any enquiry or investigation by any agency under any law:** The practice of holding an Indian citizen to ransom for acts done in a past system that was designed to be corrupt and predatory—prevents the citizen to actually reap the benefits of the new system designing itself to be anti-corrupt, and we remain always stuck in the vicious circle of corruption, despite our best efforts and intentions.
- **Incentivise wealth, instead of poverty.** The Modi government in its first term began the process by schemes like the Jan Dhan Yojana. Expecting a few honest Indians to carry the responsibility of 1.3 billion citizens is the already proven way to promote corruption, and reverse development.
- **Ensure Certainty of Punishment, Instead of Severity of Punishment.** If severity of punishment was any deterrent, murders and rapes would have been extinct. With a 3 year limitation on past investigations, all agencies Including Courts would have ample time and space to punish the guilty instead of Tareekh pe Tareekh, Tareekh ...... The declogged system would close the present avenue available to culprits to bribe their way out of the ever elusive convictions.

Thus if we will truly reform our systems to work for us, rather than the present form of against us, we will create for ourselves a much happier India.

Imagine, if instead of fighting against, fending off, and getting mentally tormented daily by disruptive government agencies, we surround ourselves with supportive, and enthusiastic government agencies whose aim is to understand our problems and issues and help us solve them, perhaps this time round we can become **The Golden Tiger.**

The Foundation for Millennium Sustainable Development Goals (MSDGs)
Contact: Ph. 011-41767867 • Deepti (M) 9717838540 • www.foundationformsdgs.com, E-mail: connect@foundationformsdgs.com

Business Standard—14 August 2019

WE ARE INDIANS AND WE ARE NOT CHORS!

For millennia, India has been the **"Golden Bird"**—सोने की चिड़िया—much looted, ravaged, lorded over, caged, and colonized by a plethora of consecutive non-Indians, who took advantage of our own petty differences that divide us from within.

Obviously, these non-Indians were more interested in their private wealth-collection, rather than the development and wealth-creation of India and Indians. A great example of this is **Robert Clive's**—the person who established the military and political supremacy of the East India Company in India—**infamous defence for the corruption charges brought against him in the British parliament**—"*…an opulent city lay at my mercy; its richest bankers bid against each other for my smiles; I walked through vaults which were thrown open to me alone, piled on either hand with gold and jewels! By God, Mr Chairman, at this moment I stand astonished at my own moderation.*"

Consequently, the systems and the laws that they created—which we have inherited are—

- blindingly opaque
- designed to amplify the farcical differences that we Indians believe differentiate us
- while putting unimaginably monopolistic and discriminatory powers in the hands of a few

On 15th August, 1947 when our parents, grandparents, and great-grandparents finally—finally took back control over our own destinies, the men and women who drafted the Constitution of India understood the enormous responsibility that they had undertaken, and so, rightly they called our democracy—**The Great Indian Experiment**.

But a lie repeated enough times begins to start sounding like the truth. For millennia, **Indians have been called thieves and criminals by those actually looting us**—so much so that we have sadly begun to believe it ourselves.

---

72 YEARS IS A LONG TIME TO BREAK THE SHACKLES OF SLAVERY—ON OUR 73RD INDEPENDENCE DAY, LET ALL INDIANS BE TRULY FREE. SAY IT WITH ME—

I AM AN INDIAN, AND I AM NOT A CRIMINAL.

Today, we have the means, the will, and the technology to make our laws, and our systems TRANSPARENT.

Let us further The Great Indian Experiment. For example let's take the Income Tax Department. How can we make it more robust, and free of corruption—

- **Abolish TAX TARGETS.** Incomes fluctuate from year to year.
    - o   Use data analysis, and data management to determine what the tax for a given period of time for every entity should be.
- Reform the duties of the **tax officers to become tax-processors**, instead of the present "tax-collectors".
- The onus needs to rest with the **tax-officer to prove, and justify the need to even communicate with a taxpayer**, let alone raid an Indian citizen's dignity without notice.
- **Harness the technology of Blockchain**
    - o   Each taxpayer using his/her unique key will be able to see the breakdown of where our tax rupees is being utilised—police, education, infrastructure, transport, health, arts, research, etc.
    - o   Because of the immutability of blockchain, any leakages enroute will be immediately identified, and addressed. Thus ensuring Certainty of Punishment.
    - o   When we Indians begin to see, and experience the benefits of our hard-earned rupees actually being utilised in public facilities that make our day-to-day lives easier, safer, and more convenient—taxes will be filed honestly, and regularly.

We already have a capable, and skilled Finance Minister, who for the first time in our democratic history began her maiden budget speech by honouring honest tax-payers—you and me. Who understands, and does not shy away from addressing the lacunae in our system.

The Modi government is actively on a **"Swachch Bharat Mission"**, taking concrete steps to deter corruption at all stages. But a nation dreaming, and endeavouring to become a $5 trillion dollar economy, cannot afford to treat and harass its citizens like common criminals.

It needs to provide the citizens a period of transition.

When the previously established system promoted corruption, and compelled citizens to navigate daily life only by paying bribes, and untoward favours to the few with monopolistic powers—the new system endeavouring to create a transparent and non-corrupt environment needs to give the citizens the time, and the confidence to live a life free of corruption.

We must understand, if there is an Indian offering and/or putting currency notes under the table, there is another Indian sitting opposite demanding and/or receiving those notes under the table too. Vilifying just one party is extremely unfair, and betrays our prejudices.

A few steps that we can take to redesign our system to be transparent and corruption-free are—

- **Put a strict 3 year limitation on initiating any enquiry or investigation by any agency under any law:** The practice of holding an Indian citizen to ransom for acts done in a past system that was designed to be corrupt and predatory—prevents the citizen to actually reap the benefits of the new system designing itself to be anti-corrupt, and we remain always stuck in the vicious circle of corruption, despite our best efforts and intentions.
- **Incentivise wealth, instead of poverty:** The Modi government in its first term began the process by schemes like the Jan Dhan Yojana. Expecting a few honest Indians to carry the responsibility of 1.3 billion citizens is the already proven way to promote corruption, and reverse development.
- **Ensure Certainty of Punishment, instead of Severity of Punishment:** If severity of punishment was any deterrent, murders and rapes would have been extinct. With a 3 year limitation on past investigations, all agencies including Courts would have ample time and space to punish the guilty instead of *Tareekh pe Tareekh*, Tareekh... The declogged system would close the present avenue available to culprits to bribe their way out of the ever elusive convictions.

Thus if we will truly reform our systems to work for us, rather than the present form of against us, we will create for ourselves a much happier India. Imagine, if instead of fighting against, fending off, and getting mentally tormented daily by disruptive government agencies, we surround ourselves with supportive, and enthusiastic government agencies whose aim is to understand our problems and issues and help us solve them, perhaps this time round we can become The Golden Tiger.

Business Standard   MUMBAI | TUESDAY, 24 SEPTEMBER 2019

Economic Downturn? Entrepreneurs are the key to Industrial Revival

The past few weeks have provided hope for Indian industry with the positive and proactive steps being taken by the Government to address the fallen economy, and the host of measures being announced to revive various sectors of the industry.

In a path breaking announcement last week, tax rates have been slashed and other tax payer friendly measures have been announced by the Finance Minister entailing a cost of Rs 1.5 lakh Crores to the budgeted revenue which would no doubt go a long way in supporting industrial development in the country and have been appreciated and welcomed by all of us. These along with various other tax reforms introduced in last few months are a clear signal by the Government of its desire to put in place a culture of honouring the tax payers and prevent undue harassment in the tax administration. But the system needs to have an inbuilt mechanism for a smooth transition from the highly corrupt past tax terrorism to a humane taxpayer friendly regime.

Because, the fact remains that the manner in which the entrepreneurial spirit has been crushed at the ground level by corrupt enforcement officials and continues to be done despite all the good intentions at government level, actual industrial revival might remain elusive and positive job creation a distant dream.

Antiquated and complicated non-compliable laws have fueled unbridled corruption leading to a mindset where corrupt conduct and practices are perceived as a birth right. This perception needs to change for things to improve. Excessive criminalization of all civil laws has led to the entire population under duress to submit to all sort of illegitimate demands whether guilty or not.

Fortunately, the current Government has very correctly identified the twin problems. It has endeavoured to repeal a very large number of old and antiquated laws in the past few years and made it very clear that it remains committed to do so on an ongoing basis. At the same time, a serious effort is being made to decriminalize the Companies Act, 2013 as far as possible. We hope that various other commercial laws would also be suitably addressed.

Despite such crackdown on old draconian laws, they continue to haunt the common Indian citizens who remain vulnerable to unlimited grave digging by all and sundry even if we have not done any wrong.

The enforcement officials have for so long been used to the old British Raj mandated oppressive ways of dealing with Indian citizens that they don't realise that the country has since been independent for 72 years now and Indians cannot and should not be treated as second class citizens in our own country. Today with change of guard at the TOP resulting in lack of immunity and much higher risk of being caught, their rates for extortion have increased alarmingly. Following their own internal rules of engagement based on "GUILTY UNLESS PROVEN INNOCENT" they find themselves free to initiate an investigation against anybody without much reasoning, and even on flimsy grounds and/or instigated by corrupt means and refuse to close any file even if they don't find anything wrong until they force a coercive confession. Otherwise, there is no end to their fishing expedition which ultimately destroys the person refusing to do so.

Despite the clampdown on corruption by the current Government, with the aid of corrupt officials, the corrupt have become much bolder and their dirty arms have reached the high pedestal of judiciary as well thereby ensuring complete immunity to them from any action by the Government.

It is high time and very urgent for our government to build accountability of each and every government official for their own actions and at the same time very urgently provide a transition period through a limitation of 3 years. This means that no enforcement agency or any other official should be allowed to enquire or investigate any act done or actions taken more than 3 years back. This would address the fear factor in every citizen's mind for anything forcibly done whether knowingly or unknowingly in the past system. ULTIMATELY, its time now to allow all Indians to say very loudly, "MICCHAMI DUKKADAM"

Allowing this transition period would also instill the confidence in the industry to gainfully utilize our resources in the growth and development of the nation instead of remaining entangled in meaningless past queries which fail to serve any purpose other than harassment and oppression. The real need is to promote more socially uplifting and exciting enterprises for EASE of DOING BUSINESS and not to allow extortion which would result in CEASE of DOING BUSINESS.

Both direct tax laws and indirect tax laws contain numerous irritants introduced with an eye on curbing tax evasion and stricter compliance which have a very negligible revenue impact but act as the fountainhead of corruption. While those indulging in such wrongs do find other loopholes to get away with cheating the system, the vast majority of tax payers are actual victims of such retrograde legislation who have to face the corrupt officials misusing such provisions for personal gains. Addressing these would certainly increase compliance across the board and reduce rampant corruption to a large extent.

To allow Indian industry successfully compete with the Chinese, there is an urgent need to reduce our transaction costs and the cost of compliance with innumerable laws and regulations which is weighing us down and throwing away our market to Chinese dominance.

The recently enacted Code on Wages, 2019 has created so many pitfalls particularly for MSMEs who seldom have a dedicated HR manager to fully understand and comply may find themselves in deep trouble. There are so many ambiguities, complexities and impractical provisions that most MSMEs may simply cease to do business. For bigger Companies, it would entail a much higher cost of compliance making them incompetitive globally. Major concern areas include definition of workman/employee, bonus to contract labour, excessive penal provisions, prosecution of MD by all and sundry, to name a few.

Besides addressing various issues and minor irritants in tax laws, the Government needs to encourage commercial decisions being taken by Bankers without fear of harassment. Some measures have been announced recently in this direction while much more is required to be done to instill a higher level of confidence in the bankers to promote honest decision making. This would go a long way in addressing the liquidity crisis in the economy and prevent many future untimely business failures, despite the businesses themselves being highly solvent and important growth pillars for our democracy.

There is a desperate need to bridge the current high level of TRUST DEFICIT and promote entrepreneurship for reigniting the much-needed industrial development in the country.

Excessive criminalization of all civil laws has led to the entire population under duress to submit to all sort of illegitimate demands whether guilty or not.

Arun Kumar Jagatramka
Chairman, Centre for Growth and Sustainable Development, FMSDGs & Group Chairman, Gujarat NRE

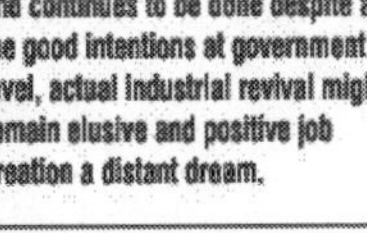

Foundation for Millennium Sustainable Development Goals (MSDGs)
C – 9/9848, Vasant Kunj, New Delhi – 110070
Email: msdgs2030@gmail.com;   www.foundationformsdgs.com

Business Standard—24 September 2019

ECONOMIC DOWNTURN? ENTREPRENEURS ARE THE KEY TO INDUSTRIAL REVIVAL

The past few weeks have provided hope for Indian industry with the positive and proactive steps being taken by the Government to address the fallen economy, and the host of measures being announced to revive various sectors of the industry.

In a path breaking announcement last week, tax rates have been slashed and other tax payer friendly measures have been announced by the Finance Minister entailing a cost of ₹1.5 lakh Crores to the budgeted revenue which would no doubt go a long way in supporting industrial development in the country and have been appreciated and welcomed by all of us. These along with various other tax reforms introduced in last few months are a clear signal by the Government of its desire to put in place a culture of honouring the tax payers and prevent undue harassment in the tax administration. But the system needs to have an inbuilt mechanism for a smooth transition from the highly corrupt past tax terrorism to a humane taxpayer friendly regime.

Because, the fact remains that the manner in which the entrepreneurial spirit has been crushed at the ground level by corrupt enforcement officials and continues to be done despite all the good intentions at government level, actual industrial revival might remain elusive and positive job creation a distant dream.

Antiquated and complicated non-compliable laws have fueled unbridled corruption leading to a mindset where corrupt conduct and practices are perceived as a birth right. This perception needs to change for things to improve. **Excessive criminalization of all civil laws has led to the entire population under duress to submit to all sort of illegitimate demands whether guilty or not.**

Fortunately, the current Government has very correctly identified the twin problems. It has endeavoured to repeal a very large number of old and antiquated laws in the past few years and made it very clear that it remains committed to do so on an ongoing basis. At the same time, a

serious effort is being made to decriminalize the Companies Act, 2013 as far as possible. We hope that various other commercial laws would also be suitably addressed.

Despite such crackdown on old draconian laws, they continue to haunt the common Indian citizens who remain vulnerable to unlimited grave digging by all and sundry even if we have not done any wrong.

The enforcement officials have for so long been used to the old British Raj mandated oppressive ways of dealing with Indian citizens that they don't realise that the country has since been independent for 72 years now and Indians cannot and should not be treated as second class citizens in our own country. Today with change of guard at the TOP resulting in lack of immunity and much higher risk of being caught, their rates for extortion have increased alarmingly. **Following their own internal rules of engagement based on "GUILTY UNLESS PROVEN INNOCENT" they find themselves free to initiate an investigation against anybody without much reasoning, and even on flimsy grounds and/or instigated by corrupt means and refuse to close any file even if they don't find anything wrong until they force a coercive confession. Otherwise, there is no end to their fishing expedition which ultimately destroys the person refusing to do so.**

Despite the clampdown on corruption by the current Government, with the aid of corrupt officials, the corrupt have become much bolder and their dirty arms have reached the high pedestal of judiciary as well thereby ensuring complete immunity to them from any action by the Government.

It is high time and very urgent for our government to build accountability of each and every government official for their own actions and at the same time very urgently provide a transition period through a limitation of 3 years. This means that no enforcement agency or any other official should be allowed to enquire or investigate any act done or actions taken more than 3 years back. This would address the fear factor in every citizen's mind for anything forcibly done whether knowingly or unknowingly in the past system. ULTIMATELY, its time now to allow all Indians to say very loudly, "MICCHAMI DUKKADAM"

Allowing this transition period would also instill the confidence in the industry to gainfully utilize our resources in the growth and development of the nation instead of remaining entangled in meaningless past queries which fail to serve any purpose other than harassment and oppression. The real need is to promote more socially uplifting and exciting enterprises for EASE of DOING BUSINESS and not to allow extortion which would result in CEASE of DOING BUSINESS.

Both direct tax laws and indirect tax laws contain numerous irritants introduced with an eye on curbing tax evasion and stricter compliance which have a very negligible revenue impact but act as the fountainhead of corruption. While those indulging in such wrongs do find other loopholes to get away with cheating the system, the vast majority of tax payers are actual victims of such retrograde legislation who have to face the corrupt officials misusing such provisions for personal gains. Addressing these would certainly increase compliance across the board and reduce rampant corruption to a large extent.

To allow Indian Industry successfully compete with the Chinese, there is an urgent need to reduce our transaction costs and the cost of compliance with innumerable laws and regulations which is weighing us down and throwing away our market to Chinese dominance.

The recently enacted Code on Wages, 2019 has created so many pitfalls particularly for MSMEs who seldom have a dedicated HR manager to fully understand and comply may find themselves in deep trouble. There are so many ambiguities, complexities and impractical provisions that most MSMEs may simply cease to do business. For bigger Companies, it would entail a much higher cost of compliance making them incompetitive globally. Major concern areas include definition of workman/employee, bonus to contract labour, excessive penal provisions, prosecution of MD by all and sundry, to name a few.

Besides addressing various issues and minor irritants in tax laws, the Government needs to encourage commercial decisions being taken by Bankers without fear of harassment. Some measures have been announced recently in this direction while much more is required to be done to instill a higher level of confidence in the bankers to promote honest decision making. This would go a long way in addressing the liquidity crisis in the economy and prevent many future untimely business failures, despite the businesses themselves being highly solvent and important growth pillars for our democracy.

There is a desperate need to bridge the current high level of TRUST DEFICIT and promote entrepreneurship for reigniting the much-needed industrial development in the country.

Business Standard MUMBAI | FRIDAY, 17 JANUARY 2020

MISUSE OF IB CODE PREVENTING POTENTIAL RECOVERY BY BANKS

FEW CORRUPT INSOLVENCY PROFESSIONALS & AUDITORS INDULGING IN EXTORTION DESTROYING THE INTEGRITY OF THE LEGAL SYSTEM

IB Code is directly and indirectly affecting almost every business in the country today, and thus it has a direct and major impact on our present state of economy. While India certainly needs an efficient and robust Insolvency and Bankruptcy Code, the manner in which the present one is being implemented and misinterpreted has not only added to the alarming slump in our economy, but has created a new avenue of corruption.

The backbone of IBC was the BLRC report which very clearly identified the role of promoters and management. The IB Code was drafted with an idea of a stand still period to allow the creditors to explore the best possible options to revive the business and maximize wealth whether with or without existing management. The legal control was handed over to the creditors to prevent any misuse by the promoters, but the promoters were acknowledged as a necessary party for the revival of the company. It did not envisage a discriminatory blanket ban on promoters at all. However, the sudden introduction of section 29A has debarred promoters and made them aliens in their own house, with no voice and representation. All business failures are treated as frauds and entrepreneurs as biggest criminals.

The worst part of IB Code is the high level of corruption that has crept in almost all parts of its implementation. The private sector professionals whether insolvency professionals or forensic auditors or valuers who have been entrusted with this very high level of responsibility have in some of the cases resorted to very high level of corruption and blackmail with no remedy in sight. There is no definition of fraud and no penalty for a malicious accusation for fraud. It's easy to accuse anybody of fraud but almost impossible for anybody to defend even if accused out of vengeance or for refusal to pay the extortion money. There is no accountability of RP or the Liquidator against any wrongdoing. The only toothless procedure is filing a complaint to IBBI which very few promoters or ousted management can dare to do.

The only people, who could understand and object to any such wrongs—the ousted promoters and/or shareholders, are not allowed any space by NCLT or NCLAT to even make any representation in the IB Code! **These professionals are perhaps the major source of high level of corruption that has even influenced a large portion of the judiciary including NCLT & NCLAT who are blindly supporting such corrupt professionals ignoring any sort of intervention by the affected stakeholders.** With most such professionals becoming rags to riches overnight with easy money that in fact belonged to the banks has led to the blatant misuse of IB Code to benefit few individuals at the cost of the entire country.

IB Code nowhere says that promoters or shareholders have no right to complaint or approach NCLT or NCLAT for their grievances but in actual practice they are not recognized and are thrown out without being heard by all 3 levels NCLT, NCLAT and The SUPREME COURT. This leaves the shareholders with no remedy despite facing blatant misuse of the IB Code by the corrupt and/or incompetent professionals.

While promoters and shareholders suffer because of their emotional attachment with the Companies created by their sweat and blood, Actually the banks and financial institutions are the real victims of such corruption as their recovery takes a back seat while these corrupt professionals loot and fill their coffers both officially as well as unofficially.

In the above backdrop, it is very urgent to recognize the role of entrepreneurs and existing management in revival of sick companies and allow the genuine ones the desired level of dignity to sufficiently voice against any wrongs being done by such unscrupulous professionals which could be the only safeguard possible against such corruption.

We must also understand that such unscrupulous professionals form a very small portion of the insolvency professionals and majority of the professionals are honest and dedicated to the core, but due to general apathy and silence of the honest majority, they are successful in taking the system for a ride. **Any crackdown on them would affect the entire profession and as such the honest majority of professionals, who could identify such wrongs before anybody else, must raise the alarm before it is too late. Few major fraudulent cases breaking out in future should not be allowed to hit the entire community through draconian measures and witch hunting of the entire profession in a manner similar to the entire promoter community being labelled as fraud because of wrongs done by a few of them.**

A very senior Banker very rightly commented—
"I think most draconian part of IBC is introduction of Section 29A. Every promoter, no matter whether they are honest or dishonest, whether the NPA is due to external or internal reasons, is barred from the process once the account is NPA. This is against natural justice. They are disallowed without giving them fair chance to prove that this is a case of genuine business failure."

However, instead of learning from past mistakes and amending section 29A to draw a distinction between genuine business failures and fraudsters; IBBI recently amended the

Arun Kumar Jagatramka
Chairman, Entrepreneurship Helpline Foundation and
Group Chairman, Gujarat NRE

liquidation regulations to debar promoters from even reviving the company in liquidation u/s 230 of the Companies Act.

The promoters were debarred during CIRP on the presumption that the company could and would be revived by any interested 3rd party but it goes for liquidation when there are no 3rd parties interested in any such revival scheme. As such, when there were no suitors for the Company during CIRP which required 66% consent of COC alone, how could one expect to have any such interest in revival u/s 230 which is highly stringent and requires 75% vote of each class of stakeholder in addition to the COC members. Debarring the promoters from this last chance to revive a company is highly disastrous.

As such, in the interest of the nation and to prevent further large-scale job losses and destruction of assets, the latest amendment to liquidation regulations, along with section 29A needs an urgent relook. Otherwise, even the last chance of reviving a company is being shut out for no fault of the various stakeholders. And without industry, there can be no economic development.

(Arun Kumar Jagatramka is a Chartered Accountant with a Gold Medal and All India 1st Rank and besides being the Chairman of Gujarat NRE group is also the Chairman of Entrepreneurship Helpline Foundation)

Advertorial

Entrepreneurship Helpline Foundation

3, New York Tower "A", Thaltej, Ahmedabad – 380054 (M) +91 8760259797, Email : entrehelpfoundation@gmail.com

MISUSE OF IB CODE PREVENTING POTENTIAL RECOVERY BY BANKS FEW CORRUPT INSOLVENCY PROFESSIONALS & AUDITORS INDULGING IN EXTORTION DESTROYING THE INTEGRITY OF THE LEGAL SYSTEM

IB Code is directly and indirectly affecting almost every business in the country today, and thus it has a direct and major impact on our present state of economy. While India certainly needs an efficient and robust Insolvency and Bankruptcy Code, the manner in which the present one is being implemented and misinterpreted has not only added to the alarming slump in our economy, but has created a new avenue of corruption.

The backbone of IBC was the BLRC report which very clearly identified the role of promoters and management. The IB Code was drafted with an idea of a stand still period to allow the creditors to explore the best possible options to revive the business and maximize wealth whether with or without existing management. The legal control was handed over to the creditors to prevent any misuse by the promoters, but the promoters were acknowledged as a necessary party for the revival of the company. It did not envisage a discriminatory blanket ban on promoters at all. However, the sudden introduction of section 29A has debarred promoters and made them aliens in their own house, with no voice and representation. All business failures are treated as frauds and entrepreneurs as biggest criminals.

The worst part of IB Code is the high level of corruption that has crept in almost all parts of its implementation. The private sector professionals whether insolvency professionals or forensic auditors or valuers who have been entrusted with this very high level of responsibility have in some of the cases resorted to very high level of corruption and blackmail with no remedy in sight. There is no definition of fraud and No penalty for a malicious accusation for fraud. It's easy to accuse anybody of fraud but almost impossible for anybody to defend even if accused out of vengeance or for refusal to pay the extortion money. There is no accountability of RP or the Liquidator against any wrongdoing. The only toothless procedure is filing a complaint to IBBI which very few promoters or ousted management can dare to do.

The only people, who could understand and object to any such wrongs— the ousted promoters and/or shareholders, are not allowed and space by

NCLT or NCLAT to even make any representation in the IB Code! **These professionals are perhaps the major source of high level of corruption that has even influenced a large portion of the judiciary including NCLT & NCLAT who are blindly supporting such corrupt professionals ignoring any sort of intervention by the affected stakeholders.** With most such professionals becoming rags to riches overnight with easy money that in fact belonged to the banks has led to the blatant misuse of IB Code to benefit few individuals at the cost of the entire country.

IB Code nowhere says that promoters or shareholders have no right to complaint or approach NCLT OR NCLAT for their grievances but in actual practice they are not recognized and are thrown out without being heard by all 3 levels NCLT, NCLAT and The SUPREME COURT. This leaves the shareholders with no remedy despite facing Blatant misuse of the IB Code by the corrupt and/or incompetent professionals.

While promoters and shareholders suffer because of their emotional attachment with the Companies created by their sweat and blood, Actually the banks and financial institutions are the real victims of such corruption as their recovery takes a back seat while these corrupt professionals loot and fill their coffers both officially as well as unofficially.

In the above backdrop, it is very urgent to recognize the role of entrepreneurs and existing management in revival of sick companies and allow the genuine ones the desired level of dignity to sufficiently voice against any wrongs being done by such unscrupulous professionals which could be the only safeguard possible against such corruption.

We must also understand that such unscrupulous professionals form a very small portion of the insolvency professionals and majority of the professionals are honest and dedicated to the core, but due to general apathy and silence of the honest majority, they are successful in taking the system for a ride. **Any crackdown on them would affect the entire profession and as such the honest majority of professionals, who could identify such wrongs before anybody else, must raise the alarm before it is too late. Few major fraudulent cases breaking out in future should not be allowed to hit the entire community through draconian measures and witch hunting of the entire profession in a manner similar to the entire promoter community being labelled as fraud because of wrongs done by a few of them.**

A very senior Banker very rightly commented–

"I think most draconian part of IBC is introduction of Section 29A. Every promoter, no matter whether they are honest or dishonest, whether the NPA is due to external or internal reasons, is barred from the process once the account is NPA. This is against natural justice. They are disallowed without giving them fair chance to prove that this is a case of genuine business failure."

However, instead of learning from past mistakes and amending section 29A to draw a distinction between genuine business failures and fraudsters; IBBI recently amended the liquidation regulations to debar promoters from even reviving the company in liquidation u/s 230 of the Companies Act.

The promoters were debarred during CIRP on the presumption that the company could and would be revived by any interested 3rd party but it goes for liquidation when there are no 3rd parties interested in any such revival scheme. As such, when there were no suitors for the Company during CIRP which required 66% consent of COC alone, how could one expect to have any such interest in revival u/s 230 which is highly stringent and requires 75% vote of each class of stakeholder in addition to the COC members. Debarring the promoters from this last chance to revive a company is highly disastrous.

As such, in the interest of the nation and to prevent further large-scale job losses and destruction of assets, the latest amendment to liquidation regulations, along with section 29A needs an urgent relook. Otherwise, even the last chance of reviving a company is being shut out for no fault of the various stakeholders. And without industry, there can be no economic development.

(Arun Kumar Jagatramka is a Chartered Accountant with a Gold Medal and All India 1ˢᵗ Rank and besides being the Chairman of Gujarat NRE group is also the Chairman of Entrepreneurship Helpline Foundation)

Business Standard   TUESDAY, 11 FEBRUARY 2020   PAGE-5

BANKERS: COMMERCIAL WISDOM Vs. COGNITIVE DISTORTION

ALL OR NOTHING SYNDROME DESTROYING COMMERCIAL VALUE

IB Code was introduced as a path breaking initiative to resolve the burning issue of large NPAs in the Banking System and empowered the Bankers to get in the Driver's seat and quickly resolve and revive the stressed Companies. A very high degree of trust was placed in the Bankers as members of COCs to decide the future of stressed Companies and maximise value thereof for the benefit of all stakeholders including themselves.

Cognitive distortions refer to thoughts which forces individuals to perceive reality inaccurately. As per Beck's cognitive model a negative outlook on reality is a major factor in symptoms of emotional dysfunction and poorer subjective well-being. Specifically, negative thinking patterns cause negative emotions.

All-or-nothing thinking is one of the many negative thought processes, known as cognitive distortions.

This cognitive distortion occurs when any judgment is based on only a portion of the information while disregarding all other information. These kinds of all or nothing beliefs can be highly detrimental to the health of our Banks as well as the economy. All-or-nothing thinking is problematic in many ways. It's limiting and "creates extreme and impossible expectations." This type of faulty thinking can also include an inability to see the alternatives in a situation or solutions to a problem.

We are well aware of the power of Positive Thinking and reviving a Company in distress requires a positive mindset and analysing all available options and deciding in favour of maximising the enterprise value.

However, despite the stress on revival as against recovery, our bankers continue to focus on recovery through all means with IB code being treated just another tool for recovery which is totally against the preamble of the Code. They have also refused to understand the onus cast on them as COC members to work towards revival of the companies. This opposition to change has been one of the chief reasons for our failure to benefit from the revolutionary IB Code.

In most cases, a company referred for resolution under the IB code is already NPA in the books of Bankers and as per existing practice, Banks shift all such accounts to their Stressed Asset Management Group which acts as the Morgue and used for recovery like harvesting of organs before the funeral. They do not have the required mindset for even running a company forget revival since supporting an operational Company is not their cup of tea.

The IB Code requires the company to be admitted to the ICU for special care which should lead to revival of the company. The moot question is How could the Company ever be revived if people entrusted with revival are only looking for doing a post mortem instead of a timely open heart surgery to save lives.

The ALL or NOTHING Syndrome prevents the Bankers from taking a practical view of the situation and revive the Company based on applicable ground realities in each situation and in their zeal to maximise recovery they actually kill the golden goose, and also destroy the wealth of the nation.

Recognising the change brought in by the IB Code, Bankers need to form a special vertical within the Bank just like, personal segment, mid corporate group, Large Corporates / CAG, Stressed Asset management group. It could be called as Corporate Restructuring/ Revival Group for handling companies undergoing CIRP. This group needs to be manned by people with Corporate Credit background and having a positive mindset. Adequate safeguards need to be built in the system to prevent any misuse as well as provide adequate protection for decisions taken based on their commercial wisdom some of which are bound to go wrong in few years' time.

This would go a long way in revival of most companies in distress and prevent Banks from booking large losses. Aiming for the moon is very good but then being imprisoned in self created Wish List Syndrome is fatal. For reducing the Bloating NPAs, industrial revival and employment generation, our Bankers need to stop Procrastinating, act faster and set in motion a decision making process based on Commercial Wisdom instead of Personal Prejudices.

(Arun Kumar Jagatramka is a Chartered Accountant with a Gold Medal and All India 1st Rank and besides being the Chairman of Gujarat NRE group is also the Chairman of Entrepreneurship Helpline Foundation)

Arun Kumar Jagatramka
@arannre

> How could the Company ever be revived if people entrusted with revival are only looking for doing a post mortem instead of a timely open heart surgery to save lives.

Letter from a young daughter to her industrialist father

The Roots of the Black Money problem in India

Anthony J. D'Angelo says, "When solving problems, dig at the roots instead of just hacking at the leaves":

In our current efforts to make India a global economic powerhouse, we have certain challenges which need to be surmounted. One of these challenges is the Black Money stashed by Indians in various tax haven countries.

As a young Indian studying in Ahmedabad, I remember seeing this issue crop up in the papers time and again, but could never understand the need for people to keep their money outside India in other countries. Wasn't it better invested in the various financial schemes offered by public as well as private institutions in India? Why do these individuals feel the need to hide this cash? Answers to such questions remained a mystery to me then.

A few years after I joined my father, his company faced financial difficulties due to its correlation with the world steel sector. My father being the promoter along with company executives started working with the various bankers towards restructuring proposals and other options. I was able to be a part of such discussions and noticed that at such meetings the bankers would request my father as promoter to infuse cash into the company.

This request would always puzzle me, the bankers had first charge over all the company assets, shares etc. as well as signed personal guarantees from the promoters listing all their personal assets as well. Then what more other outside cash were they requesting?

At one meeting, my father seemingly tired of the repeated demands very categorically said, "*I have never kept any separate cash outside India and do not plan to do so in the future as well*". The penny dropped.

How can a promoter be expected to have free cash, unaccounted to the tax authorities when his company is in dire situation? If he does have this cash, does it not mean that he allowed the company's operations to go bad, while at the same time filling his own coffers? Is this not Black Money that is plaguing India?

After that day, I see news article after article where promoters have gone with restructuring proposals only to receive the answer to infuse cash in the company in exchange for support. Does this mean that the system is trying to punish these promoters for not having black money? Are such promoters being penalised because they have declared all their assets in an honest manner?

Sometimes, I think that the black money stasher individuals were smart, and saw this future need for hidden funds, and maybe my father should have done the same, but then I think what would have been the price. To do so would mean, not to believe in India and its growth story. To consider other countries more safe then our own country, India.

But I BELIEVE IN INDIA.
Let's make sure that MAKE IN INDIA does not turn out to be SELL INDIA.

We do need stricter monitoring and must punish any promoter who has taken out cash from the Company that he is supposed to nurture and protect but at the same time identify and honour the few honest ones and rather allow them to revive their companies with dignity which could set an example for others. Ultimately, the nation must be able to trust its people.

Advertorial

Entrepreneurship Helpline Foundation

73, New York Tower "A", Thaltej Ahmedabad - 380054 (M) +91 9280259792. Email: entrehelpfoundation@gmail.com

Letter written by my younger daughter Kavita

Business Standard—11th February, 2020

BANKERS: COMMERCIAL WISDOM VS. COGNITIVE DISTORTION ALL OR NOTHING SYNDROME DESTROYING COMMERCIAL VALUE

IB Code was introduced as a path breaking initiative to resolve the burning issue of large NPAs in the Banking System and empowered the Bankers to get in the Driver's seat and quickly resolve and revive the stressed Companies. A very high degree of trust was placed in the Bankers as members of COCs to decide the future of stressed Companies and maximise value thereof for the benefit of all stakeholders including themselves.

Cognitive distortions refer to thoughts which forces individuals to perceive reality inaccurately. As per Beck's cognitive model a negative outlook on reality is a major factor in symptoms of emotional dysfunction and poorer subjective well-being. Specifically, negative thinking patterns cause negative emotions.

All-or-nothing thinking is one of the many negative thought processes, known as cognitive distortions.

This cognitive distortion occurs when any judgment is based on only a portion of the information while disregarding all other information. These kinds of all or nothing beliefs can be highly detrimental to the health of our Banks as well as the economy. All-or-nothing thinking is problematic in many ways. It's limiting and "creates extreme and impossible expectations." This type of faulty thinking can also include an inability to see the alternatives in a situation or solutions to a problem.

We are well aware of the power of Positive Thinking and reviving a Company in distress requires a positive mindset and analysing all available options and deciding in favour of maximising the enterprise value. There is no room for procrastination and any delay in decision making not only destroys value but also makes revival that much more difficult.

However, despite the stress on revival as against recovery, our bankers continue to focus on recovery through all means with IB code being treated just another tool for recovery which is totally against the preamble of the Code. They have also refused to understand the onus cast on them as COC members to work towards revival of the companies. This

opposition to change has been one of the chief reasons for our failure to benefit from the revolutionary IB Code.

In most cases, a company referred for resolution under the IB code is already NPA in the books of Bankers and as per existing practice, Banks shift all such accounts to their Stressed Asset Management Group which acts as the Morgue and used for recovery like harvesting of organs before the funeral. They do not have the required mindset for even running a company forget revival since supporting an operational Company is not their cup of tea.

The IB Code requires the Company to be admitted to the ICU for special care which should lead to revival of the company. The moot question is How could the Company ever be revived if people entrusted with revival are only looking for doing a post mortem instead of a timely open heart surgery to save lives.

The ALL or NOTHING Syndrome prevents the Bankers from taking a practical view of the situation and revive the Company based on applicable ground realities in each situation and in their zeal to maximise recovery they actually kill the golden goose, and also destroy the wealth of the nation.

Recognising the change brought in by the IB Code, Bankers need to form a special vertical within the Bank just like, personal segment, mid corporate group, Large Corporates / CAG, Stressed Asset management group for handling companies undergoing CIRP under the IB Code which could be called as Corporate Restructuring/Revival Group. This group needs to be manned by people with Corporate Credit background and having a positive mindset. Adequate safeguards need to be built in the system to prevent any misuse as well as provide adequate protection for decisions taken based on their commercial wisdom some of which are bound to go wrong in few years' time.

This would go a long way in revival of most companies in distress and prevent Banks from booking large losses. Aiming for the moon is very good but then being imprisoned in self created Wish List Syndrome is fatal. For reducing the Bloating NPAs, industrial revival and employment generation, our Bankers need to stop Procrastinating, act faster and set in motion a decision making process based on Commercial Wisdom instead of Personal Prejudices.

LETTER FROM A YOUNG DAUGHTER
TO HER INDUSTRIALIST FATHER

The Roots of the Black Money Problem in India

Anthony J. D'Angelo says, *"When solving problems, dig at the roots instead of just hacking at the leaves"*.

In our current efforts to make India a global economic powerhouse, we have certain challenges which need to be surmounted. One of these challenges is the Black Money stashed by Indians in various tax haven countries.

As a young Indian studying in Ahmedabad, I remember seeing this issue crop up in the papers time and again, but could never understand the need for people to keep their money outside India in other countries. Wasn't it better invested in the various financial schemes offered by public as well as private institutions in India? Why do these individuals feel the need to hide this cash? Answers to such questions remained a mystery to me then.

A few years after I joined my father, his company faced financial difficulties due to its correlation with the world steel sector. My father being the promoter along with company executives started working with the various bankers towards restructuring proposals and other options. I was able to be a part of such discussions and noticed that at such meetings the bankers would request my father as promoter to infuse cash into the company.

This request would always puzzle me, the bankers had first charge over all the company assets, shares etc. as well as signed personal guarantees from the promoters listing all their personal assets as well. Then what more other outside cash were they requesting?

At one meeting, my father seemingly tired of the repeated demands very categorically said, *"I have never kept any separate cash outside India and do not plan to do so in the future as well"*. The penny dropped.

How can a promoter be expected to have free cash, unaccounted to the tax authorities when his company is in dire situation? If he does have this cash, does it not mean that he allowed the company's operations to go bad, while at the same time filling his own coffers? Is this not Black Money that is plaguing India?

After that day, I see news article after article where promoters have gone with restructuring proposals only to receive the answer to infuse cash in the company in exchange for support. Does this mean that the system is trying to punish these promoters for not having black money? Are such promoters being penalised because they have declared all their assets in an honest manner?

Sometimes, I think that the black money stasher individuals were smart, and saw this future need for hidden funds, and maybe my father should have done the same, but then I think what would have been the price. To do so would mean, not to believe in India and its growth story. To consider other countries more safe than our own country, India.

But I BELIEVE IN INDIA.

Let's make sure that MAKE IN INDIA does not turn out to be SELL INDIA.

We do need stricter monitoring and must punish any promoter who has taken out cash from the Company that he is supposed to nurture and protect but at the same time identify and honour the few honest ones and rather allow them to revive their companies with dignity which could set an example for others. Ultimately, the nation must be able to trust its people.

Appendix 2

POWERPOINT PRESENTATIONS

Few slides from the presentation done in February 2009 to highlight
'Link between Corruption and Terrorism'.

Note—
The original complete presentation with all photos may be downloaded from **www.selfiewithintegrity.com.** You can also send an email to **selfie@gujaratnre.com** with **'Link between Corruption and Terrorism'** in the subject line.

12 March 1993

Bomb blasts in the Bombay Stock Exchange

- Serial blasts
- Hijacking of aircrafts
- Loss of innocent lives
- Attack on the Parliament
- Defiling places of worship
- Gun battles ...

India has mourned innumerable times

She has picked up her dead and wounded to move on only to be targeted again

But the point is not about impotency of the state

★ Point is, some patriotic Indian had taken a bribe to let the consignment of RDX through

★ Others had been "bought" & "purchased" on the way

★ Still others had used loopholes in the antediluvian legal system to protect and shelter him

★ Other Indians had, for political reasons, either looked the other way, or had actively encouraged his metamorphosis

➡ **The laws of the land are antiquated**

➡ **The enforcers are corrupt**

➡ **The law makers are politically motivated**

And the people morally bankrupt

26 November 2008

It's the small bribe that "we" pay

That let's them buy the guns that are trained on us

The *Hawala* route that we take

To evade a few Rupees … is used by them to finance their operations around the world

Few slides from the presentation
done in May 2009 to highlight
'Ill Effects of Corruption'.

Note—
The original complete presentation with all photos
may be downloaded from **www.selfiewithintegrity.
com.** You can also send an email to **selfie@
gujaratnre.com** with **'Ill Effects of Corruption'** in
the subject line.

The founding Fathers had lovingly given her, her colours

Saffron indicating courage and strength

White indicating peace and truth

Green indicating fertility, growth and auspiciousness

But, After five decades of freedom

We still remain, Hindus and Muslims;
Madrasi's and Marathi's and Bihari's;
Dalits and Brahmins ....

In the great land of India,
there being no true Indian

A Nation

Where greasing the palm is not an exception, but the rule

Individually

We are up against a "system" that is naturally averse to change,

for maintenance of status quo ensures :

equitable distribution of bribe,

thriving of vote banks, continuity of personal fiefdoms,

reign of the corruption

The Genesis lies in

The sense of depravity of justice and lack of transparency in transactions

We refuse to nip a problem in the bud, allowing it to escalate

Judiciary is gasping under the combined pressures of anachronistic laws & Inefficient execution which leads to infinite delays – both procedural and practical

Which in turn

- Creates alienation and hatred

- Erodes faith in the system

- Forces otherwise honest people to be corrupt

Injustice Breeds Corruption

Why *me* ? We all ask

**As it is easier to shrug,
pay the price
and move on,
than be the victim of
"the system"**

Few slides from the presentation done by a student for a contest organised by Gujarat NRE group in December 2009 to highlight **'Does Corruption Feed Terrorism'**.

Note—

The original complete presentation with all photos may be downloaded from **www.selfiewithintegrity.com.** You can also send an email to **selfie@gujaratnre.com** with **'Does Corruption Feed Terrorism'** in the subject line.

Does Corruption Feed Terrorism?

How Can We Get Rid of Such Corruption

By Mansi OZa

N.L. Dalmia Institute of Management Studies and Research

Corruption

- Corruption is lack of Integrity
- It could be financial, moral or intellectual integrity
- The corruption temperature of any society depends on three factors :
  - ❑ The individual sense of values
  - ❑ The values cherished by society
  - ❑ The system of governance

Corruption & Terrorism – A nexus

- Corruption is
  - ➢ Anti national
  - ➢ Anti poor
  - ➢ Anti economic development

All three of these leads to flourishing of terrorism in the society.

Hawala scam showed how anti-national Kashmiri militants were getting money from abroad, the same route through which other sections of the society like politics, business and bureaucracy were also receiving money.

Terrorism is further bolstered by this nature of corruption.

Terrorism — The three elements

- ❖ Foundation
- ❖ Financing
- ❖ Breeding

Terrorism - Foundation

- Corruption encourages physical acts of terrorism. Militant activity in the North East and in Jammu and Kashmir can be directly linked to the extensive and pervasive corruption in these places
- GOI has been consistently throwing a lot of money in an effort to promote development in these states but thanks to corruption, the legitimacy of the formal state is compromised and the militants gain greater public sympathy and legitimacy

Corruption thus plays a substantial role in foundation of terrorist activities.

Terrorism — Financing

- Drug trafficking: 321 billion USD
- Human trafficking: 10 - 15 billion USD
- Illicit arms trafficking: 2 -10 billion USD
- Hawala
- Piracy
- Charities

All these activities flourish only in a corrupt society—A corruption free society will paralyze these sources of financing and hence terminate terrorism.

Terrorism — Breeding

- Higher corruption incidences triggers more youth to indulge in terrorist activities
- Higher corruption leads to rapid spreading of terrorist activities
- Higher corruption leads to greater and easy expansion of terrorist organizations

Address corruption or terrorism ?

- Corruption is pre-requisite for all 3 elements of terrorism
- To kill terrorism from its roots, corruption must be ended
- A well planned & sustained attack on corruption will lead to better & terror-free world

---

Understanding roots of corruption and terrorism

- Cultural and social roots
  - Culture of tolerance
  - Sinner gets redemption by enchanting Narayana during his last few moments
- Vicious circle and prestige needs
  - Belief that power is an opportunity to a mass wealth and hence abuse power
- Growing consumerism
  - Desire to have best lifestyle at the start of career
  - To earn wealth by hook or crook or even corruption
- Social Pressure
  - Family needs
  - Low salaries of government employees — Leading to substandard lifestyle

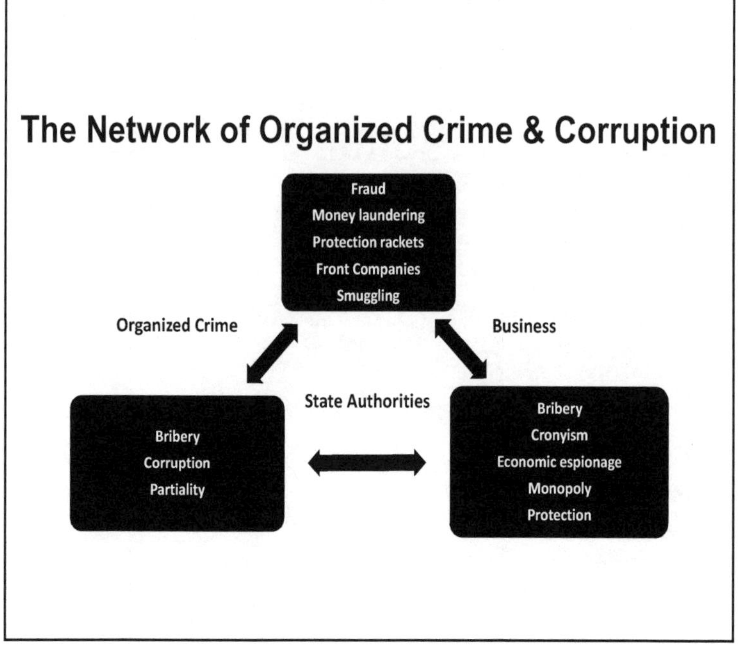

Unaccounted money in India is estimated to be in the range of Rs.550 to 600 thousand crore more than the combined revenue of the Centre and the state government in the last fiscal.

Solution — The Three pillars

- A solution has to encompass all the elements of the society to generate a sustainable and effective solution to eradicate corruption

Individual   Organization   Agency

Individual

- **Educating the importance of ethics**
    - The society will be corruption free if every individual decides to maintain highest standard of ethics
    - Implementation of education systems and subjects which promote highly ethical standards
    - Roadshows and demonstrations to promote ethical business
    - Explaining the effects that corruption has on the society

- **Setting examples**
    - Awards to recognize ethical workers
    - Setting Up initiatives to promote ethical behavior

- **Initiation of a full fledged "Ethical India" program**

Ethical India Program

- **Television and Radio**
    - Television and radio shows to address corruption
    - Commercials inspiring anti-corruption feeling in youth
    - Shows and contests to recognize and appreciate ethical behavior

- **Public showdown and moral attack on corrupt officials**

- **Initiatives in all the offices where corruption is rampant**
    - Inspirational seminars
    - Motivation programs
    - Addressing and implementing views of officers which can eradicate corruption

- **Internet**
    - Blogs and website forums to recognize ethical behavior and promote it as well as attack corruption
    - Pop-ups to promote ethical behavior

Fighting corruption - Agencies

Judiciary

In its recent judgments the Supreme Court has enunciated 3important principles, which will go a long way reduce corruption.

Constitution is supreme and it expresses people's will

- Corrupt politicians who claim that they have been acquitted in highest court, namely   people's court in elections can no longer claim that

- Special provision in the Constitution to the effect that a person who is not member of legislature can be made a minister for 180 days cannot be invoked more than once

- Clear judgment in case of Chief Minister often pointing out that a person, who is not eligible to contest elections, cannot be sworn in as a minister

Fighting corruption - Agencies

Bodies like the CVC, CBI, anti-corruption bureau, vigilance commissioners in the state

The recent case in Delhi where the issue of corruption to the extent of the Rs.4o crores per month indulged in by the police and the municipal officials by collecting bribes from the hawkers, vendors and rickshaw pullers was resolved clue to the act of Madhu Kishwar, an activist from NGO Manushi.

Print and electronic media

- To publicize cases of corruption and policies that encourage financial terrorism

Direct action

- The action taken by Lok Satta, an NGO in Andhra Pradesh to expose the extent of tampering of meters in petrol pumps and corrupt practices

Few slides from the presentation done in September 2011 to highlight
'The Need to Trust the Citizens'.

Note—
The original complete presentation with all photos may be downloaded from **www.selfiewithintegrity.com.** You can also send an email to **selfie@gujaratnre.com** with **'Compliance in an Ethical Society'** in the subject line.

Compliance in an Ethical Society: Trust Based or Enforced

Rich Vs Poor Nations

- **Distinction between civilizations is not a fall out of age, natural resources or demographics**

What matters is ATTITUDE…

Attitude is Everything  **Attitude changes everything**

Principles adhered to by the people of the Rich & Developed Countries

- Ethics, as basic principles
- Integrity
- Responsibility
- The respect for Laws and Regulations
- The respect for citizens by right
- The love for work
- The effort to save and invest
- The will to be productive
- Punctuality

WE ARE WANTING IN ALL OF THE ABOVE

WE LACK ATTITUDE…

WE ARE IN THIS STATE BECAUSE
WE WANT TO TAKE ADVANTAGE OVER
EVERYTHING AND EVERYONE

WE ARE IN THIS STATE BECAUSE
WE SEE SOMETHING DONE WRONG
AND SAY - "LET IT BE"
CHALTA HAI

WE SHOULD HAVE A SPIRITED
MEMORY AND ATTITUDE...

ONLY THEN WILL WE BE ABLE TO
CHANGE OUR PRESENT STATE

We are still under a colonial Seize

We inherited a partitioned India as a slave's legacy with corruption packaged free – with shackles in the mind for next 60 years

Need to get rid of the Prisoner Mentality & the Mental Block

We are still following laws framed Centuries ago – Laws which are impractical and need an urgent relook

> **SOME UNIQUE CASES OF BAD LAWS, IMPRACTICAL LAWS, UNCOMPLIABLE LAWS – LEADING TO EXTORTIONARY CORRUPTION....**
>
> **UNBRIDLED EXTORTIONARY CORRUPTION ULTIMATELY LEADS TO AND ENCOURAGES COLLUSIVE CORRUPTION**

> ## Vague and impractical laws make all of us culprits
>
> In developed countries there is a border within which you need to operate. Violation amounts when you cross the border.
>
> In India you have to walk on a straight line. No one can walk on a straight line, making all guilty in one way or the other.

- This gives the enforcement agencies a free hand to pick whom so ever they wish

- Giving enormous scope for the enforcement agencies to exercise their power

- Resulting into thriving of extortionary corruption

KITNE KHOON MAAF, SAMBA…??

- Highest tax paying Bollywood actress gets hounded by taxmen at 7 am in the morning

- Presence of an actor is the 'masala' story enjoyed by all

No one questioned why the taxmen went there at that time?

Is Paying High taxes a crime in this country as the Tax Dept's slogan CATCH the BIG FISH seems to suggest

The Effect of Enforced Compliance

"Rule of law has been replaced by rule of men"

We do not see convictions

- guilt is proven by raids
- media feasts on 'breaking news'
- the person is put in jail and released in a few days without any trial

There is no compensation- but the loss of reputation is irreparable

Fear of Raids much greater than Raids itself

The Raid Raj

During the pre-independence era, the police used to raid households at odd hours in search of freedom fighters and harass them at the slightest pretext

In India today, we have the same story repeated …

only the backdrop has changed

Enforcement agencies bulldoze their way in organizations and households, harass the common man taking recourse to some

impractical laws and walk out with their pockets full….

Even after 60 years of independence, we are shackled by these redundant laws and we have no way to fight our way out of it …

The Raid Culture: An International Perspective

- No tax raids in nations like Australia, US or UK
- Taxpayers are not treated like terrorists/drug peddlers.
- Govt's assumption on voluntary payment of taxes is appreciable and result oriented
- Hence, the tax compliance level is much higher as compared to us
- Successful because of the fact that there is certainty of strict punishment for the defaulters unlike a freeway for those with pockets full of black money.

Non-compliable provisions in most revenue legislations…….

- Lead to all being defaulters - differing only in scale
- Big evaders can afford to buy the system out
- While genuine ones are unable to match the payout of tax evaders to keep the officials happy
- Leading to even the genuine ones turning into evaders in the longer term

It is also a result of…..

Preconceived Mindsets like –

"Everybody evades tax"

Which even forces the honest to be corrupt

- Which discourages the honest to pay higher tax……
- Leading to more leakage……
- Multiple division of entity…etc….

And Justice for All... ???

"India has become a nation of 'gestures', the fundamental problems are not dealt with, only a few gestural actions are taken to cover up a deeper rot".

"The nation is happy to live in lie, deceit and dishonesty and we have all chosen to become hypocrites".

Certainty of Punishment as Against Severity of Punishment

- The Guilty should not be allowed to roam scot free
- Certainty of Punishment would deter others from repeating the mischief
- "Certainty of Punishment" is not espoused by our judicial system. Focus is rather on "Severity of Punishment"
- More severe the punishment, higher the payout of bribe

We need to come out of the...

**Age old mentality of the
Oppressed and the Oppressor....**

**Where the enforcement agencies are
viewed as the oppressor**

And the common man as oppressed

**The British have left but
have left the legacy of Class behind**

'kasauti investigation ki'

Timely closure of all investigations

**Investigations in India tend to
continue like soap operas... a
never ending saga of twists and
turns without a definite end in
sight..**

**Files are opened or pending based
on who is in power**

The Men in Power...

Have easy access to those enforcement agencies and bend the law with impunity

While the common man grapples for Justice

Injustice Breeds Corruption

- **Creates alienation and hatred**
- **Erodes faith in the system**
- **Forces otherwise honest people to be corrupt**

Corruption is:
- **Anti National**
- **Anti Poor**
- **Anti Development**

The Enforcement Agencies...

- **Need to be Empowered, Independence in operation**
- **Trained & Paid Well**
- **So that they may act accordingly to enjoy the faith of the local populace**
- **Need to enthuse more trust in us, the common men, and become more approachable**
- **Key to bring back the faith in the men in uniform who give their lives to save us**

The 2nd Freedom Struggle has already started

Freedom From Corruption and Harassment

Few slides from the presentation done in
September 2012 to highlight
**'Governance Deficit Derails
the Freedom Run'.**

Note—

The original complete presentation with all photos
may be downloaded from **www.selfiewithintegrity.
com.** You can also send an email to **selfie@
gujaratnre.com** with **'Governance Deficit Derails
the Freedom Run'** in the subject line.

THE DEFICIT SAGA...

FISCAL DEFICIT

ETHICAL DEFICIT

INTEGRITY DEFICIT

TRUST DEFICIT

And the Mother of All

GOVERNANCE DEFICIT

Corruption – Do we care?

- **Corruption has become the most discussed word in recent times - on TV debates, newspapers and drawing room conversations**
- **However it has not deterred the corrupt nor has it reduced corruption**
- **Because, we ignore the corrupt around us**

- **The big question is - Do we realise that corruption is one of the prime reasons for all the evils around us?**
- **Real change is to move the issue further from Ram Lila Maidan & Jantar Mantar and the evening debates - to the way we behave, the manner we react to events around us and the way we transact**

More Laws ?? Aren't there enough?

- Governance is not about enacting more legislations and formulating regulations
- Enough of laws - some archaic and antiquated as one may put, should be scrapped or made relevant
- It is more of implementing the legislations & regulations in its true spirit
- Any number of legislation being framed or regulators appointed, would not usher Good Governance, if there is an all encompassing disregard in following and implementing them

India at 65   Governance in freeze

- We have well defined rights but lack in well prescribed duties, so that the corrupt can be held accountable when breached
- Those who govern us:
  - Do not have <u>specific</u> duties or responsibilities (duties are vague and more like broad vision statements)
  - Do not have constitutional obligation cast on them
- To protect the revenue derived from the taxes we pay
- To defend us from internal & external threats
- To serve us & provide the basic necessities
- We do not have a legal benchmark, listing the punishment when they fail to deliver the above

India at 65... How free is Indian Enterprise?

- A manufacturing unit needs to comply with nearly 70 laws & regulations
- Even to comply with the multiple laws & regulations one has to fill forms each of around 20-30 pages and undertake multiple visits to various government offices
- File as many as 100 returns in a year and face multiple inspections
- More the touch-points & complication, corruption flourishes and its tentacles sharpens

India at 65.. Unshackle the Indian Enterprise...

- Policy making being changed with retrospective effect
- Recent trend of rules and regulations becoming regressive
- Clearances given in the past being reversed in the name of environment protection and inclusive policies
- Investor confidence at its ebb
- A country where about 70% of population lives below $2 a day, preservation of wild life is given more priority than feeding the millions — a case of misplaced priority or is there more to it - harassment leading to greater corruption??

India @ 65.. Corruption in Unison

Non-compliable provisions in most revenue legislations.......

- Lead to all being defaulters - differing only in scale
- Big evaders can afford to buy the system out
- While genuine ones are unable to match the payout of tax evaders to keep the officials happy
- Leading to even the genuine ones turning evaders in the longer term

India @ 65
Growth at Incubator battles Corruption

- Land, Natural Resources, Airwaves, are all imperative in today's business – having complete government control over them makes honest business impossible
- When an economy grows, some sectors are likely to grow faster – slight manipulation in regulatory or licensing rules in these sectors result in windfall gain for a handful
- Mutually enhancing collusion – a syndrome that is inflicting detrimental blow on our economy which is at the initial throes of development

India @ 65.. Inspector Raj still in full swing…

- License raj may be over but some of its vestiges rule - IT, Excise, Police, X, Y, inspectors force their way
- As the debate of discretion and allocation rages
- Tension between parliamentary supremacy and the rule of law remains unsolved
- Investments, similar to Politics is getting regionalized – even big business houses feel the heat of state level politics

India @ 65.. Raid Raj mentality reigns

- During the pre-independence era, the police used to raid households at odd hours in search of freedom fighters and harass them at the slightest pretext
- Today Enforcement agencies bulldoze their way, harass the common man taking recourse to some impractical laws and walk out with their pockets full….
- The backdrop has only changed – white masters replaced by brown sahibs

The Raid Raj (Red Raj)

Sadly though…

The Raid Raj has led to the proliferation of the Red Raj that has affected the nation at large and is one of the most burning issues of today

---

The Raid Culture : An International Perspective

- No tax raids in developed nations like Australia, US or UK
- Taxpayers are not treated like terrorists/drug peddlers.
- Govt's assumption on voluntary payment of right amount of taxes is appreciable and result oriented
- Hence, the tax compliance level is much higher as compared to us
- Successful because of the fact that there is certainty of strict punishment for the defaulters unlike a freeway for those with pockets full of black money.

India @ 65
Rule of law replaced by rule of men

We do not see convictions

- **Guilt is proved by raids**
- **The person is put in jail and released in a few days without any trial**
- **There is no compensation- but the loss of reputation is irreparable**
- **Fear of Raids much greater than Raids itself**

India @ 65.....All's (not) Well

- **Fear of India moving to a new Hindu <u>growth rate</u> (the low annual growth rate of the <u>economy of India</u> before the liberalisations of 1991) of 5-6% much less than the 9-10% "Chindia" (a portmanteau word that refers to China and India together in general) dream**
- **Corruption is morally abhorrent and evokes popular revulsion**
- **Hurts the Nation economically as policy paralysis precipitates**
- **Fear of any supposed wrongdoing leading to bureaucratic inaction**
- **The Aam Aadmi suffers as welfare of poor is only possible from revenue generated through overall economic growth**
  - **Fewer jobs & more unemployment**
  - **Strain on welfare projects**

India @ 65....We need to....

- Be more assertive – by quietly acquiescing, we become party to corruption
- Must make our views heard
- Must support those who stand and try to fight corruption
- Individually oppose corruption wherever we find it

India @ 65....... The call is for...

- More transparency & lesser touch points with government agencies
- Simplification and digitalization
- More of e-governance, online filling of forms, applications & returns
- Less of multiple-level interfaces and
- TRUST

The problem is in attitude and a belief that – one in business must be doing some wrong

Extortionary & Collusive Corruption

Extortionary	Collusive

Extortionary

* The common man and the poor most hit
* Forced primarily by government bodies and enforcement agencies
* Citizen has no choice - ends up losing time/money /opportunities if denies the bribe
* Less talked about and not highlighted by media since sum involved in individual cases is much less though adds up to a humungous total

Collusive

* Paid to public authority to fleece the general public
* Eg. Government Contracts, tenders, projects, etc.
* Loser is the general public as cost of public service goes up and efficiency goes down
* All big scams that we hear about are of this type
* Does not affect the common man in his day to day life

WHILE COLLUSIVE CORRUPTION IS LIKE DIABETES THAT CAN ONLY BE CONTAINED AND CANNOT BE ELIMINATED;

EXTORTIONARY CORRUPTION IS A BANE TO UNDERDEVELOPED NATIONS & CEASES TO EXIST AS IT TRAVERSES A PATH OF GROWTH TO DEVELOPED....

We had to shell out 'pranami' for telephone connection, gas connection or for certain consumer durables like a scooter or even a car until few years back- UNKNOWN TO POST '91 GENERATION

20

Few slides from the presentation done in December 2015 to highlight **'Ease of Doing Business'.**

Note—

The original complete presentation with all photos may be downloaded from **www.selfiewithintegrity.com.** You can also send an email to **selfie@gujaratnre.com** with **'Ease of Doing Business'** in the subject line.

Why do I....

- Throw my garbage with merry abandon?

- Spit in free will, as if without that one right I would be a citizen of a lesser democracy?

- Tear off a page from a library book or write my name on the Taj Mahal?

- Leave a public toilet smelling even though I would like to find it squeaky clean as I enter it?

- Why is my sense of Public hygiene so porcine?

Why do I....

- Jump red lights with the alacrity of a jackrabbit leaping ahead of a buckshot?

- Block the left lane, when my intention is to turn right?

- Overtake from the left?

- Drive at night in the city with the high beam on?

- Jump queues with the zest of an Olympic heptathlon gold hopeful?

Why are we the way we are? 

- We can not shrug off the fact that we use much of our intelligence to figure out ways of circumventing every law, regulation, and norm in a bid to do better for ourselves
- To twist and turn every available opportunity and prospect to our immediate advantage
- Arising more from the "What can I do" or "How does it matter if I do not follow" syndrome
- We forget that it is not just I but many I's' becoming WE, to effect the change from the way we are at present

….(Un)fair Competition

- It is easier to pull someone down than to pull someone up
- We discourage fair competition and have in many fields tried to create barriers for foreign investment which would have increased efficiency
- We need to create a transparent and conducive environment
- We also need to understand that to attract foreign investment we need to get out of our obsession on what we can get out of them– there are no free lunches… investment in business is for profit and not for charity

Is Doing Business in India a Crime??
GUJARAT NRE
• Majority of business want to be Honest
• But is there any business today that can vouch that it has been honest throughout?
• Why is it that the majority of businesses have been subject to corruption – primarily extortionist corruption?
• Why have we built a system that makes doing business honestly in India so tough?

GUJARAT NRE
EXTORTION
That Industries face on a regular basis

THE ROOT OF CORRUPTION AND CHAOS

- Parallel roads and covered drainages – seems to have went out of fashion with Mohenjo-Daro and Harappa
- Today, we just erect buildings haphazardly and hope that in due course we will be able to carve out a road through the mess
- This defect in behavior and approach lies at the root of our filth, corruption and chaos

Extortion by local politicians

- The local politicians find industry as an easy target for their benefit
- They put pressure on industry for
  - Employment of their supporters as workers/employees
  - Use of vendors associated with them for any outsourced job like transportation, material handling and other contractual jobs
  - Or by acting on frivolous complaints to extract benefit in cash or in kind

Extortion of enforcement officials

- Industries are subject to extortion of enforcement officials like Factory inspector, Labour inspector, environment/pollution officials
- The antediluvian laws of the land has many such provisions which can be referred by the enforcement agencies at their will to harass
- No industry in the country can claim to be 100% compliant with all the bad provisions in various laws that govern us

Bribes Extortion & Business

License Raj gone but Inspector Raj still thrives

- Visit of any of these inspectors would not conclude without a consideration
- Any unsubstantiated complaint is enough to raise a query culminating in a demand
- Industry generally tends to acquiesce to such unlawful demand only to avoid further harassment
- Excessive power in the hands of enforcement agencies are one of the greatest impediments to the ease of doing business

Industry viewed as a cash cow

- Local politicians want industry to set up in their area and then milk them for their benefit
- They at times act as local mafias
  - Any outsourced or contractual work if not awarded to their firms results in disruption of work
  - The firms associated to local politicians do not act professionally and are at times not commercially viable
  - The syndicate managed by the local politicians are against the interest of the business and industry

Exploitation of Alienation

- Naxalites in large parts of the country thrive on giving local populace the false sense of protection against land encroachment and by speaking for tribal rights
- They have exploited the sense of abandonment among Adivasis caused by the apathy of administration since independence towards the development of large tribal lands, which still remain undeveloped and cut out from mainstream
- They have thrived on the false sense of Adivasis of being 'have-nots', as well as alienation and apathy of the disadvantaged rural poor

Political extortion leading to Naxalism in tribal areas

- Naxalites thrive in tribal areas known for mining activity
- Where there is mining there is conflict of tribal rights – a soft issue to gain popular support
- Naxalites however do not see mining and allied industry as an enemy, but a source of illicit revenue
- Industries operating in Naxalite prone area are forced to pay protection money to conduct business

Rich Vs Poor nations

Distinction between civilizations is not a fall out of age, natural resources or demographics

What matters is ATTITUDE...

ATTITUDE IS EVERYTHING  ATTITUDE CHANGES EVERYTHING

Extortion remains the backbone of Indian economy

- Naxalites do extortion through use of arms and by operations that is unlawful
- The extortion happening in non-Naxalite area is different only by the kind of people and ideology of the person
- The extortion is the same. Industry is the victim and is forced to pay in both the instances

- **Majority of businesses want to be Honest**
- **But is there any business today that can vouch of being honest throughout?**
- **Indian businesses are subjected to FORCED CORRUPTION**
- **Corruption is today in our DNA**

WHEN WE ANALYSE THE CONDUCT OF THE PEOPLE FROM THE RICH AND DEVELOPED COUNTRIES, IT IS OBSERVED THAT MOST ABIDE BY THE FOLLOWING PRINCIPLES OF LIFE

- Ethics, as basic principles
- Integrity
- Responsibility
- The respect for Laws and Regulations
- The respect for majority of citizens by right

- The love for work
- The effort to save and invest
- The will to be productive
- Punctuality

WE ARE WANTING IN ALL

WE LACK ATTITUDE...

I am Proud To be An INDIAN

We need to Rediscover Ourselves....

Rediscover ourselves as a Proud Indian

We need to Change the Way We Are

More Laws ??
Aren't there enough?

- Governance is not about enacting more legislations and formulating regulations
- We have enough of laws - some archaic and antiquated
- Should be scrapped or made relevant
- It is more of implementing the legislations & regulations in their true spirit

THE ARCHAIC PROCESSES

- Existence of innumerable laws imply that the focus is more on the process of executing the law rather than principles
- And, laws that document process only complicate doing business in India
- Obscure and ridiculous laws fuel corruption
- There is a strong negative correlation between levels of corruption and business accessibility

The problem lies in

- Too much of regulations
- Archaic laws that have lost relevance
- Discretionary powers vested on individuals
- A colonial mentality of continuing with laws for subjects
- Disregard to the basic principle that tougher the law, more the violation leading to greater corruption

Leading to greasing of palm...

Street level corruption affects the Common Man the most

We continue to be under a colonial seize

We have inherited a partitioned India as a slave's legacy with corruption packaged free – with shackles in the mind for next around 70 years

Need to get rid of the Prisoner Mentality & the Mental Block

We are still following laws framed Centuries ago – Laws which are impractical and need an urgent relook

Law of majority

- Corporate sector is forced to face corruption as a cost to do business in India
- Democracy runs on the law of majority
- Today, when the majority of businesses are labeled as corrupt, the entire country becomes corrupt
- This majority should be given a chance to come clean and do a honest business

Need for a Radical Approach 

- The new government has the mandate, intent and the willingness to bring the required change
- Need to avoid knee-jerk reactions and criminality provisions that would make all of us criminals
- Need to review each regulation, its use, misuse and its relevance
- Need for systemic changes or a major surgery to rectify the system – An uphill task, but it is NOW or NEVER

Second Freedom Struggle 

- Need for a comprehensive exercise to build a system which Trusts the Citizens
- Need to drastically change the regulations that have the colonial legacy
- Need a revolutionary approach for freedom from Laws of the British Era
- The laws that were framed by the British to treat Indians as slaves and subjects of the Queen

Incorruptible Indians

We need to identify and honour Incorruptible Indians instead of hounding them to death or oblivion which is done in the current system.

India needs an army of Incorruptible to identify the nation as a Superpower.

Police Reforms

- Archaic and colonial police laws of 1861 – to suit the needs of the then British masters to tame Indians
- Today we need a Police force to serve Indians
- An approachable and friendly police force required to sharpen the intelligence mechanism
- Credibility deficit – instill a sense of trustworthiness in police among citizens at all times

Labour Reforms

- Indian labour laws are numerous, complex and even ambiguous—promote litigation rather than the resolution
- Archaic laws discourage hiring, is counter productive for workers for whose welfare it is designed
- Over-regulated labour market

Land Reforms

- The Land Acquisition Bill 2013 is discouraging and does not meet the purpose
- Is likely to create more problems than confusion—make manufacturing expensive and scarce
- Cost of land acquisition to increase many fold
- Thanks to competitive politics, land reforms is stuck—the country suffers

Companies Act 2013: Need for a New Act

- This is a new addition to the already mesh of laws that are non-compliable and makes business difficult
- The act needs to be nullified and replaced by a newly drafted pragmatic Companies Act at the earliest

Effective Governance

- Amend CrPC and make registration of Crime more user-friendly & easy
- Judicial reforms, independent appointment of judges
- Introduction of shift system of cases
- Speedy disposal of cases by the courts and other authorities so that delay and secrecy do not allow corruption to breed
- Reclassify crimes so that minor offences could be addressed through plea bargaining
- Execute wholesale electoral reforms and regulate functioning of political parties

Fight against Black Money

- Identify the causes of existence of Black Economy—like degree of controls & regulations, etc.
- A complete overhaul of tax system with a bold message to encourage self-compliance
- Black Economy is a threat to security of the country – fight against black economy should be more for peace and stability than revenue
- Discourage and remove extortionary corruption
- Focus on black money in lockers of Indian banks

Real Estate
The REAL Story is BLACK within

- Black Money in Real Estate can vanish overnight
  - Exemption of Capital Gains Tax
  - Reduction in stamp duty to 1%

No Incentive for Black Money involvement

Overall gains by removing Black Money from Real Estate deals is much more than the notional loss due to zero capital gains tax & lower stamp duty

Don't compel people to be corrupt, rather encourage them to be participatory

The problem may be that Corrupt politicians & Officers may find it hard to park their black money elsewhere.

KITNE KHOON MAAF, SAMBA...??

- Highest tax paying Bollywood actress gets hounded by taxmen at 7 in the morning
- Presence of an actor is the 'masala' story enjoyed by all
- No genuine effort to remove or penalise black money in Bollywood

No one questioned why the taxmen went there at that time?

Is Paying High taxes a crime in this country as the Tax Dept's slogan CATCH the BIG FISH seems to suggest?

Honour the Large Tax Payers 

- o Need to come out of 'Catch the Big Fish' mentality
- o Honour the large tax payers and stop hounding them
- o A list of large tax payers in a city (top 10) /state (top 50)/ country (top 200) may be published and honoured
- o This is similar to business rankings and would encourage others to be large taxpayers and enter the coveted ranking by just peer pressure
- o Encourage people to be compliant rather than coercing them

Non-compliable provisions in most revenue legislations.......
GUJARAT NRE
• Lead to all being defaulters - differing only in scale
• Big evaders can afford to buy the system out
• While genuine ones are unable to match the payout of tax evaders to keep the officials happy
• Leading to even the genuine ones turning into evaders in the longer term

'kasauti investigation ki'
GUJARAT NRE
Timely closure of all investigations
Investigations in India tend to continue like soap operas...a never ending saga of twists and turns without a definite end in sight...
The Guilty Needs to be Punished

Certainty of Punishment as Against Severity of Punishment

- The Guilty should not be allowed to roam scot free
- Certainty of Punishment would deter others from repeating the mischief
- "Certainty of Punishment" is not espoused by our judicial system. Focus is rather on "Severity of Punishment"
- More severe the punishment, higher the payout of bribe

Let us all Build a Society on the Foundation of TRUST

"We must learn to Trust. For several centuries, Indians have been brainwashed to distrust other Indians. This saps national energy. Distrust kills initiative. Distrust compels people to maneuver and manipulate. Trust and transparency stimulates entrepreneurship."

Few slides from the presentation done in April 2016 to highlight **'Time to Change—Ease of Doing Business'**.

Note—

The original complete presentation with all photos may be downloaded from **www.selfiewithintegrity.com.** You can also send an email to **selfie@gujaratnre.com** with **'Time to Change—Ease of Doing Business'** in the subject line.

Time to Change

**We need to Change the Way We Are...
Rediscover ourselves as a Proud
Indian...
We need to Rediscover Ourselves...**

Mr Arun Kumar Jagatramka
Chairman,
ASSOCHAM National Council on Ease of Doing Business
Chairman and Managing Director, Gujarat NRE Coke Ltd

(DIS) EASE OF DOING BUSINESS IN INDIA

Why Is Doing Business a Crime??

- Is there any business today who can vouch that it has been honest throughout?
- Why are majority of businesses subjected to corruption – primarily extortionist corruption?
- Have we built a system that makes doing business honestly in India so tough?

What Ails the System?

- Too much of regulations
- Archaic laws that have lost relevance
- Discretionary powers vested in individuals
- A colonial mentality of continuing with laws for subjects
- Tougher the law, more the violation leading to greater corruption

THE ARCHAIC PROCESSES

➤ Existence of innumerable laws imply that the focus is more on process of executing law rather than principles
➤ And, laws that document process only complicate doing business in India
➤ Obscure and ridiculous laws fuel corruption
➤ There is a strong negative correlation between levels of corruption and business accessibility

---

Need to get rid of the Prisoner Mentality & the Mental Block

We are still following laws framed Centuries ago—Laws which are impractical and need an urgent relook

---

Land

Absence of an effective land acquisition process has made land acquisition very complex and time-consuming

Labour

Existing restrictive labour laws have hampered the business growth and inflow of foreign investment in India as well as catalyzed labour unrest

There is no free Lunch

Taxes: Direct & Indirect

Overly complicated tax systems have encouraged evasion and are associated with larger informal sectors, more corruption and less investment

We don't need a tax 'heaven' neither do we want a tax 'hell'

An ideal tax structure is one where cost of evasion is more than compliance

Taxes: The Solution

- Immediate implementation of GST
- Reduction in number of ambiguous taxes
- Abolition of discretionary powers of the tax officials
- _Stop tax raids_- no place in a civilised society, but they continue because officials like the power it gives them over the richest men in India, and also the extra money earned
- Avoid multiple taxation regime
- Ambiguity / Overlap in Custom Duty/ Service Tax and VAT
- Incentives to the industry facing bias in indirect tax regime
- Increase in accountability of tax officials

Honour the Large Tax Payers

- Need to come out of the 'Catch the Big Fish' mentality

- Honour the large tax payers and stop hounding them

- A list of large tax payers in a city (top 10) /state (top 50)/ country (top 200) may be published and honoured with annual VVIP status

- This is similar to business rankings and would encourage others to be large taxpayers and enter the coveted ranking by just peer pressure

- Encourage people to be compliant rather than coercing them

Regulatory & Compliance issues

Majority of business houses want to do business the noble way but are compelled to take recourse to some kind of corruption due to the existence of widespread extortionary as well as collusive corruption resulting from too much of regulations and laws that have lost relevance

Public Servants – need for accountability

- Arbitrary assessments which are ultimately struck down on appeal causes unnecessary heartburn and an opportunity for the assessing officer to harass till the case is settled
- Or demand money by way of extortion for not doing an arbitrary assessment
- There should be some penalty or accountability on the assessing officer for doing arbitrary assessments which are ultimately struck down on appeal
- This is very much required so that assessee is not the only who is penalized for arbitrary assessments and this would refrain the officer from making it a tool to blackmail

Regulatory & Compliance Issues: The Solution

- **Promote trust based compliance**
- **A large section of backlog of cases is due to multiple appeals by government officials**
- **Accountability should be fixed on the officials for appeals made in higher courts against unfavourable judgements**
- **There is a cost associated with each appeal and govt. officials should not be penalised for accepting the verdict if it goes against them.**

Regulatory & Compliance Issues: The Solution

- **Zero tolerance to non-compliance and certainty of punishment is a deterrent to the sibling effect**
- **All investigations and filing of complaints should be done within a maximum of 3 years**
- **Decision on cases should be declared within one year unless any extraordinary circumstances**
- **Specifying timelines for approvals and 'silent is consent' clause**

Dilemma of How & Why – reforms in backgear

- Scams should not deter liberalisation process
- In past liberalisation has been negated by reaction to each scam
- Over zeal to plug HOW the scam happened, resulted in extra regulation, tightening the system and more laws
- We need to analyze WHY it has happened and *Rectify the Root Cause*

We did not analyse Why Satyam happened

Instead, on analysing How it happened, attempt was made to paint all NIFTY 100 companies in the same brush - Enquires were ordered

The changing approach to business by our leaders

- We today are fortunate to have a government which is willing to change
- A government which has shown intent to break out of the sloth and is open to suggestions for change
- Acknowledges the challenges faced by the industry
- Receptive to suggestions to bring growth back on track
- Need to now end the cat and mouse game between the government and the industry

Let us all
Build a Society
on the
Foundation of TRUST

"The only way to make a man trustworthy is to trust him."

Few slides from the presentation done in September 2016 to discuss **'Bankruptcy Code and S4A** (Sustainable Structuring of Assets)'.

Note—

The original complete presentation with all photos may be downloaded from **www.selfiewithintegrity. com.** You can also send an email to **selfie@ gujaratnre.com** with **'Bankruptcy Code and S4A'** in the subject line.

A noble attempt

- **The government needs to be applauded in trying to bring about the much needed insolvency code**

- **Has tried to address important failings of the past**

- **It has attempted in introducing one comprehensive law for corporate insolvency**

- **It sets a time frame of 180 days for insolvency resolution, with a 90-day extension if judged necessary, to be followed by liquidation**

- **However, absence of some significant provisions takes the sheen off an otherwise much-needed reform**

Challenge of Misuse and Mischief

- A single small creditor (operational or financial) can make an application to initiate corporate insolvency
- While the major creditors might be working out a revival plan, the small creditor having no stake in revival may force liquidation to the detriment of creditors and stakeholders
- To safeguard the interest of all creditors – Basic minimum requirement should be - 50% or 60% creditors needed to trigger the code
- This is required to stop misuse and mischief

Challenge of Sudden Bankruptcy

- Sudden bankruptcy may lead to lot of MISTRUST and DIFFICULTY in doing business
- Sudden bankruptcy may result in other creditors caught off-guard
- Creditors who have extended credit recently would get a raw deal
- Unsecured creditors would not get the chance to progressively work out ways in recovering a part of the debt

Misuse by Unscrupulous Promoters

- **Unscrupulous Promoters may also misuse the system by filing an application to initiate corporate insolvency**
- **Initiation of corporate insolvency process would provide relief to such unaccountable promoters against any existing legal proceedings or arbitration**
- **The bankruptcy code should not provide anyone with an easy way out to avoid the rule of law or become a means for misappropriation or funds**

Tilted in favour of creditors

- **Tilts heavily in favour of creditors, depriving debtors of fair participation and a level playing field**
- **The code does not even require the corporate debtor to be heard before ordering the commencement of proceedings and the takeover of the management and debtors' powers by the insolvency professional**
- **It is contrary to principles of natural justice and not conducive to the business environment of the Indian economy.**

Sustainable Structuring of Stressed Assets (S4A)

CDR -why it failed

- A surge in reference to CDR cell was noticed in 2012-13 and 2013-14
- Today there are hardly a few successful exits from CDR because:
  - Restructuring was often done just to delay the classification of an account as NPA rather than making efforts to make it viable
  - The interest of banks is in maintaining the account as standard instead of ensuring revival and sustainable operations
  - The expected upturn in the economy did not materialise during 2014 – 2015 which was crucial to success of CDR cases
  - The large number of companies turning NPA and failing in CDR proves that the ailment was not at promoters end but at a more systemic issue governed by the external economic environment
  - Most CDR cases were half-baked solutions with short-term solution instead of longer term revival plans

SDR - Could not take off

- SDR or strategic debt restructuring was invoked in a few companies but it did not succeed
- It is not the job of the banks to run a company nor it is easy to get so many strategic investors for the huge number of companies who are in this crisis
- A new management oblivious of the challenges and complexities of the business would not have the magic wand to bring a turnaround
- Is unjust to hang existing management for problems due to industry wide recession

S4A - Too late and Half-baked

- This should have been announced a year ago when most CDR cases were on the verge of failure
- Would have then saved the banks and the financial system from the crisis that it is faced with today
- Most of the stressed accounts have already turned NPA
- The current scheme needs to be more flexible to be effective and workable – Half-baked solutions do not help in times of crisis

The dilemma of half – Sustainable and unstainable

- The 50% criteria may result into certain inefficiencies or overstretching
- A debtor whose sustainable debt can be more than 50% may restrict it to 50%
- A debtor whose sustainable debt is less, say, 40% would stretch it to 50% to fall in the scheme, which ultimately may result into failure of the entire exercise
- Instead, the sustainable debt may be carved out based on an independent TEV study and final decision taken by the high powered committee looking at best possible options

Need for more flexibility for success

- Elbow room in deciding the repayment schedule – may be allowed to stretch if needed to match the future cash flows
- Flexibility in lowering loan rates, since interest rate are trending down
- Encouragement for banks – The portion of sustainable debt may be allowed to be treated as standard. This would act as a huge impetus for banks to make it a success

Few slides from the presentation done in February 2017 to discuss
'Ease of Doing Business in India—Recommendations'.

Note—

The original complete presentation with all photos may be downloaded from **www.selfiewithintegrity.com.** You can also send an email to **selfie@gujaratnre.com** with **'Ease of Doing Business in India—Recommendations'** in the subject line.

FM says Indians are Tax Non-Compliant

- **Are Indians non-compliant by nature or is the system non-conducive for compliance?**
- **Onus of motivating people to become compliant lies with the government**
- **Need to bring down cost of compliance**
- **Need to come out of the chicken and egg problem - tax base should be increased first or the tax rates lowered**
- **Current system has not changed things in last 70 years – need to try out something different**

Making India Tax Compliant

- Reduce tax rates drastically:
  - <u>Personal Tax</u>
  - 5 to 10 lacs - 10%   10 to 50 lacs - 15%
    50 to 100 lacs - 20%   Above 100 lacs - 25%
  - <u>Corporate Tax</u> – Maximum of 18%
  - No surcharge or any other hidden tax as well as no exemptions
- Lower tax would increase compliance as evasion would not be lucrative
- Other benefits associated with lower taxes like savings, consumption, demand and growth would result in higher tax collection

Discretionary powers of tax officers

- The recent budget allows reopening of old cases of over 10 years
- This would lead to higher corruption
- Stop Tax terrorism – which has risen after demonetization
- Enable a culture of honest tax paying citizens – People are not tax evaders by nature, but are afraid of the myriad tax laws and the litigations

Accountability of Tax officers

- The Finance Bill 2017 suggests an amendment in the IT Act with retrospective effect to insulate the tax officials
- Gives protection to tax officers from scrutiny
- It only increases the fear of arbitrary behaviour
- It is contrary to the governments' agenda of a tax-payer friendly administration
- Unbridled power in the hands of tax officials would only abate corruption

Need for accountability of Public Servants

- Arbitrary assessments which are struck down on appeal should be stopped
- Penalty or accountability must be on the assessing officer for arbitrary assessments which are ultimately struck down on appeal
- This would ensure that assesse is not penalized by arbitrary assessments and would refrain the officer from making it a tool of blackmail

Accountability at all levels

- Officials are questioned if they do not appeal against an unfavourable order – this needs to change as a policy through government order
- Instead, accountability should be fixed on the officials for appeals made in higher courts against unfavourable judgements
- Government officials should be protected by law and not penalised for accepting the verdict if it goes against them
- This would reduce the overload on Judiciary

Harassment of the Honest

- Demonetization has not changed the scenario
- Tax officials are today busy maintaining a diary of amount that people owe to them in new currency
- It is only a change in the color of currency for them

Suggestions : Direct Tax

- **Suitable modification in provisions of the IT Act is required so that the assessing officer can not reopen a case 3 years from the end of the financial year**
- **Also, the assessing officer shall not reopen a case unless tangible material proof is brought to table which proves that certain income escaped assessment**
- **Any judgement delivered by a tribunal or a High Court in favour of an assesse can not be disregarded and the adjudicating authorities should follow the precedents of the higher authorities when facts are same**

Suggestions – Concept of Materiality

- **Introduction of the Concept of Materiality in our revenue collections while dealing with small amounts in dispute**
- **Revenue laws should allow forego of relatively small amounts (1% or less value of the transaction) in dispute**
- **The demand notice should be sent based on the quantum of tax already paid – someone who has paid Rs.50 crore tax, should not be harassed with a dispute of say, Rs.50 lakhs**

Example of Saga of less than 1%

Case 1

- Coking coal imported = 1.23 lakh tonne
- Customs Duty paid = Rs.4.73 crore
- Demurrage charge = Rs.15.55 lakhs
- Customs duty on demurrage which is under dispute = Rs. 84,000/-
- Dispute as a % of total duty paid = 0.02%
- Cost of Harassment = Huge

Case 2

- Coking coal imported = 7.29 lakh tonne
- Customs Duty paid = Rs.36.89 crore
- Floating Crane Charge = Rs.6.68 crore
- Customs duty on Floating Crane charge which is under dispute = Rs.34.74 lakhs
- Dispute as a % of total duty paid = 0.94%
- Cost of Harassment = Huge

Bureaucratic Corruption

- There is no end to summons, notices and surveys
- There is no end to documents called for examination in surveys
- Conclusion is not reached in any of the issues—only to be picked and harassed at will

Bureaucratic Corruption

- Harassment continues till greasing of palm
- Industries at times prefer to complete the transaction at the initial stages to avoid long drawn harassment
- There is no end to such bureaucratic interference in sight as State monitoring and meddling in individual free space as well as with individual liberty is on the rise

Is Corruption their Birthright?

- The tax administration process and the officials involved in tax collection are the biggest source of black money
- Tax officials feel corruption as their birthright
- You are harassed if you resist payment
- Business disruption is a collateral loss
- Complaints are often handled by their superior officers who is more corrupt and feels annoyed by your complaint

Made in the USA
Monee, IL
07 July 2026